ST. TERESA'S CASTLE OF THE SOUL:

A Study of the Interior Castle

St. Teresa's Castle of the Soul

A Study of the Interior Castle

by Father Peter Bourne, H.M.C.
of the Hermits of Mount Carmel

WENZEL PRESS

BOOKS BY THE SAME AUTHOR:

Oh Happy Venture: A treatise on Carmelite Prayer
(Wenzel Press, 1992, paper)

St. John of the Cross and the Dark Night:
Understanding His Ascent and Dark Night
in Easy Stages (Wenzel Press, 1993)

Homilies for Living the Faith
(Wenzel Press, 1995)

BX
2179
.T4
M722
1995

The chapter in this book entitled, *"Man, the Image of God,"*
was first published by *Spiritual Life Magazine* in 1963 by ICS
Publications, 2131 Lincoln Road, N.E., Washington, DC 20002

Library of Congress Cataloging-in-Publication Data

Bourne, Peter, 1929–
    St. Teresa's castle of the soul: a study of the Interior castle/
by Peter Bourne.
        p.   cm.
    Includes bibliographical references.
    ISBN 0-930887-19-0 : $19.95
    1. Teresa, of Avila, Saint, 1515-1582. Moradas. 2. Spirituality—
—Catholic Church——History——16th century. 3. Catholic Church—
—Doctrines——History——16th century. I. Title.
BX2179.T4M722   1995
248.4'82--dc20
                                                      94-31700
                                                         CIP

Write for a free catalog to:

WENZEL PRESS
P. O. Box 14789-B
Long Beach, CA 90803

DEDICATED TO:

My sister, Joan of the Cross,
The Carmelite Nuns,
and
Carmelite Contemplatives,
both lay and Religious

Contents

Seventh Mansions: Spiritual Marriage

PART II
DOCTRINAL STUDIES

Prologue

St. Teresa of Jesus was born in March in the year 1515. This puts her under the sign of the Ram. I do not adhere to the science of astrology, but we can't deny that there are definite traits of personality which seem to fit each of these categories. In one article treating of the signs of the zodiac, it says: "Arians have as their symbol the new-born baby contemplating his own fingers and toes. Born leaders, always at the head of things, always taking charge, they are direct, courageous, volatile and as powerful as an atom blast; they are also inclined to be belligerent and egotistical. Arians are well qualified generals and empire-builders.

This description certainly fits St. Teresa's character. She was a born leader, courageous, and concerned for a time over the impression she made on others. And like most people, it is hard to separate her character from her accomplishments. Moreover, God has a way of making use of a person's talents, as long as that person cooperates with his grace. It was her role in life to become a Reformer, and a guide in the ways of the spirit. Today she carries the title of Mother Foundress of the Discalced Carmelites, and "Doctora" of the Church mainly because of her exalted writings. Ironically, neither of these accomplishments were initially contemplated. Her first "house of the Reform" (St. Joseph's in Avila) was the result of her desire to simplify, and return to the roots of Carmel. She had no other plans. As we know the thing mushroomed. Her vocation as a writer also was unplanned; her confessors and superiors commanded her to write.

Having studied the Spanish language and literature, together with the history of Spain, especially the period in which St. Teresa lived, it is my opinion that one needs to put St. Teresa in historical perspective in order to better understand her writings and relate them to our own times and problems, which in many ways parallel our own. She was surrounded by circumstances which are terribly familiar to us in this period of renewal.

The Council of Trent was convened seven years after she entered the Carmelite Order, and it endured for 21 intermittent years, that is from 1542 to 1563. St. Teresa's first foundation in Avila was made just one year before the Council ended. What I have found so interesting is the fact that neither St. Teresa nor St. John of the Cross referred excessively to the Council in their writings. I don't think we should conclude, though, that the Council had no effect on their lives. St. Teresa's *Constitutions* for her nuns was the result of the Council decrees. Each Council requires a certain "renewal." But it must be pointed out that the real renewal of the Church began some years before the Council. Their Catholic Majesties (Ferdinand and Isabella) received a Bull from Pope Julius II as early as 1494 to reform the Religious Orders of their realm. We can say, similarly, today's renewal also began before our Council (Vatican II) with the encyclicals of Pope Pius XII, or even those decrees of St. Pius X. Spain was in a period of gradual renewal up to and including the Council of Trent. It was at this time that translations of the great theologians and mystical writers of the Middle Ages were made into the vulgar tongue. This naturally caused renewed interest in spiritual matters, and eventually produced a school of mystical writers which surpassed them all, especially in the writings of St. Teresa and St. John of the Cross.

Simultaneously, with the rise of mysticism, there also was a new "humanism" taught in the Universities, mostly through the influence of Erasmus. Because of the widespread corruption in the Church, there was through this humanism a movement towards a greater simplicity, away from ceremony and toward an interior religion, and a desire to return to the faith and practice of primitive Christianity. These same sentiments were at the base of Luther's revolt against authority. Teresa had been in a monastery eleven years when Luther died in 1546, and the unrest, dissension and the liberal ideas he provoked found their way into Spain. Luther had translated the Scriptures into German in 1522. This gives us some idea of why the Church in Spain was so defensive against "spiritual movements," the vernacular, and any challenge of authority. The reconquest of Spain from the Moors had been a 800-year campaign, so the Spaniard was no stranger to accommodation and ecumenism. But now the shoe was on the other foot; to be Spanish was to be Catholic and the country had no desire to repeat what they had so hard earned.

Many of the issues of Vatican II had been the same as those of Trent. Trent handled them definitively, and threatened censure to all dissidents. Vatican II attempted an accommodation to the world of these same ideas, and thus far has shied away from enforcement of its decrees.

St. Teresa was at the beginning of this disunity of the Church. She seemed to be God's gift to the Church and an example of how to handle such an unpleasant situation. Her initial idea, as we know, was to form an intimate little group of friends of God, so that God would have someone to rely on as his Body was being rent asunder. Her renewal was of her own personal life first. She proposed not something new and experimental, but rather a return to the sources; she wanted to imitate those early hermits on Mount Carmel. The limitations placed on Church structure did not allow her to conform to the hermit life physically, but it did not prevent it spiritually, which was the more important element anyway. She did not fall back on Council documents to attain her ideal as we do today. Physically, she would not have found them much help, but spiritually they gave her the certitude of Faith she needed.

Councils come and go; the truths of the Faith are the same, and the Gospels should be our primary guide in what we do. Thus far our Council has failed to deliver that promised renewal. If anything, we are showing signs of spiritual bankrupcy, either because we have been more concerned with structure and relevance or because we have failed to oppose the forces of evil, and chosen comfort and accommodation instead of walking the way of the Cross. This is the path that St. Teresa outlines in her writings. But first and foremost, she points to the dignity of the human person—that each person possesses a spiritual soul made in the image and likeness of God. This is especially true of her work, the *Interior Castle*, which is an exposition of the human soul in its quest for the recovery of its life with God before the Fall. This is the renewal that we should all be concerned with. For as Our Lord said, "What does it profit you, if you gain the whole world and lose your immortal soul?"

In this work, my basic treatment is of the *Interior Castle*, which is the result of a series of lectures given to the members of the Association of Our Lady of Mount Carmel, a Third Order, under the direction of the Hermits of Mount Carmel of Lemhi,

Idaho. To gain the full benefit of this book, it is suggested that one read the chapters of St. Teresa's work along with this text. I have introduced the *Interior Castle* with a few chapters of explanation of St. Teresa's writings, and in Part II, I have included a serious study of the soul as the "image of God" and the abode of the Most Holy Trinity according to the insights of St. Teresa in her *Interior Castle.*

I have consulted both major translations of St. Teresa's works: the one by E. Allison Peers, and the other by Frs. Kieran Kavanaugh and Otilio Rodriquez. But I have relied entirely on my own translations from the *Obras Completas* of Fr. Tomas de la Cruz, OCD. I have purposely kept them literal to capture some of her literary style which is sometimes disjointed.

It was St. Teresa, herself, who gave this work we are considering the title, *Castillo Interior.* She wrote it on the back of the first page of the original; and here she also refers to it as a treatise for her sisters and daughters. However, in Spain it still goes by the name of *Las Moradas.* This is taken from the chapter headings, where St. Teresa uses *Moradas* (always in the plural) for each division, one through seven.

It has always been a difficulty in translating *Las Moradas* into English. Fr. Kieran preferred to use *Dwelling Places*, which is correct, but not very poetic. E. Allison Peers used the more familiar *Mansions. Mansions* is a legitimate translation of *moradas*, though not as exact, and it is taken from St. Teresa's reference to St. John XIV, 2, where the Lord tells his disciples that "in my Father's house there are many *mansions.*" The Latin Vulgate uses the word *mansiones*, which in the older translations of the Bible was *Mansions.* The newer ones use either room or dwelling.

In my work I have preferred to use *Mansions* to distinguish it from the many *rooms* in each. Moreover, St. Teresa used another word for these rooms: *aposentos* she called them as distinguished from *moradas.* Except for the different stages, I have not been overly concerned about the use of singular or plural of *mansions.*

Hopefully by reading this work of mine, you will find some small help in going to the original works of St. Teresa, who could claim an inspiration far superior to any I have had.

Introduction to the Writings of St. Teresa

St. Teresa is, perhaps the widest known woman saint in the Church. To those who have any acquaintance with her at all, she is also one of the most appealing personalities that ever lived, and this personality seems to shine through every page of her numerous writings, even in translation. We can surmise, then, what she is like in her original tongue. As E. Allison Peers has said: "To Spaniards there is no writer whose personality communicates itself with greater immediacy and intensity than does that of St. Teresa—and this both because of her almost complete disregard of the literary conventions, and because in nothing that she wrote could her strong individuality ever be concealed" (Vol. I, Works, p. xiv).

With this in mind, it is our intention and our hope to present St. Teresa to you, not so much from the anecdotes of her life, as from the writings which she has left us which reveal a substantial spiritual doctrine and a good glimpse of herself. (I will treat in this chapter of her writings—where they were written, when and why—as a sort of brief introduction, and in a second chapter, I would like to speak of her literary style.)

First, to give us some framework in which to locate her, St. Teresa was born on March 28, 1515. At the age of 21 she entered the Convent of the Incarnation—a large convent having a hundred or more nuns. From this date, 1536 to 1560, when she took her first steps toward founding a house of reform, she lived what would appear an ordinary life of a nun in the 16th century. She has said that she accepted no offices (Life xxxv,7). "I was never a friend of any office—on the contrary, I had always refused them." And among the papers belonging to the Convent of the Incarnation there is no record of her holding an office. This, in itself, seems extraordinary—that she attained the age of 45, with all her talents, without the so-called "honors" of office. She simply was not interested in honors of this type, and later on, as Mother Reformer, grasped the true meaning of Christian leadership as an office of service. She founded her first house of the Reform in 1562 on August 24th, and in the ensuing years, a dozen or more others. She died on October 4th, 1582 at the age of 67. Her period of writing extended over a span of 22 years, that is, from 1560, after she had experienced a few extraordinary mystical phenomena in the form of visions, until the very year of her death, when she added the final chapters of her *Foundations.*

St. Teresa wrote four major works and they are: her autobiography, called simply *Life* after the Spanish *el libro de la vida.* This is the first of her works and it usually occupies the first place in all the collections of her works. There is some evidence that St. Teresa wrote a rather extensive work some years before this in the form of a confession. She says, "I began to deal with my general confession and to put in writing all the good and bad points that I understood and knew without leaving anything more to say. I remember as I looked at it, after I wrote in it so many bad points and almost nothing good that it gave me the greatest anguish and affliction" (Life xxiii, 15).

This confession was given to a young Jesuit, Father Diego de Cetina, and, since it was under the seal of confession, he probably burned it in his cell after reading it. We have no way of knowing how long it was.

The other major works are: *The Way of Perfection*, or in Spanish: *Camino de perfection; Book of the Foundations (el libro de las fundaciones)*, and her most perfect work, *The Interior Castle.* In Spain it is known as *Las Moradas* or the *Mansions.* St. Teresa gave it the title of *Castillo Interior* (interior castle) and divided it into *moradas* (mansions) instead of chapters. The fuller title should be *Las Moradas del Castillo interior* (the mansions of the interior castle). Also it is of note that St. Teresa left each of the seven mansions in the plural—because there are many rooms in each mansion.

Some authorities would include the work, *Conceptions of the love of God*, among her major works because it has seven chapters. This work is called *Las meditaciones sobre los cantares* in Spanish. (I will explain this later.)

If we include this work just mentioned, there are nine minor works of the saint, plus her poetry and the many letters she wrote.

The other eight are:

1. *Spiritual Relations* or *cuentas de consciencia* (in Spanish, which means manifestations of conscience)
2. *Visitation of Convents of the Nuns*
3. *Constitutions of the nuns*
4. Maxims *(written for her nuns)* (avisos)

Three tiny works entitled (according to Peers):

5. *Thoughts and Maxims of St. Teresa of Jesus.* The Spanish edition calls it simply *Apuntaciones* (or notes)
6. *Judgment given by St. Teresa upon various writings on the words "Seek thyself in Me"*
7. *Answer of St. Teresa of Jesus to a Spiritual Challenge (Desafio)*
8. *Exclamations* (or Meditations) of the soul to God.

In the Spanish edition of her complete works is included a small writing called *Statutes for a Confraternity*, presumably written by St. Teresa. With the inclusion of this work there is expressed the satisfaction of the editor that St. Teresa made contact with the ordinary people (a thing we hardly have to worry about!).

Another book which has thought to have been written by St. Teresa is the work *Seven Meditations on the Pater Noster* (not to be confused with the extract taken from her *Way of Perfection*, which has been printed as a separate book). This work of the seven meditations is a pious commentary on the Our Father, and has no resemblance to St. Teresa's style. It was mistakenly included among her writings in a 1630 edition but has been excluded ever since.

One last (or rather first) work of the saint which is no longer extant may have been a novel written when she was very young. This is entirely plausible and it is mentioned by Padre Ribera, her first biographer. St. Teresa, following the "bad example" of her mother, read avidly (along with the rest of Spain) the books of chivalry then in vogue. So popular were they and so insipid, that Cervantes composed his all-time novel, *Don Quijote*, to poke fun at them. We can be assured if St. Teresa and her brother wrote such a novel, she was also responsible for destroying it.

There is not the same difficulty in reaching accurate copies

of St. Teresa's works as there is, for instance, in obtaining those
of St. John, because we have original and signed copies of all
her works, thanks to King Philip who requested them for his
library in the Escorial. There, one can see the *Life*, the *Way of
Perfection*, the *Foundations* and the *Method for the Visitation
of Convents*. An autographed copy of the *Interior Castle* is now
at the Carmel of Seville. There is also a second copy of the *Way
of Perfection* in the possession of the nuns at Valladolid. The
only confusion comes from the many faulty copies which were
made by inexact scribes, along with the difficulty of deciphering
St. Teresa's handwriting in the originals. This has been overcome
by the publication of critical works in Spanish.

The first person to edit the works of St. Teresa was the
most learned and famous biblical scholar of his day, Fray Luis
de Leon (an Augustinian). He is also Spain's foremost lyric
poet, ranking next to St. John of the Cross in the purity of his
poetic vision. This edition did not include all the works we have
today. One notable exclusion was the *Foundations* because
many of the people mentioned in the work were still alive at
the time; it was thought to be premature to publish it. Also it
lacked the minor works except for the *Relations*, *Maxims* and
the *Exclamations*.

Now I would like to locate a little more accurately these
writings of St. Teresa. But first we may ask why did St. Teresa
write at all—did she consider it her vocation to be an author as
well as a reformer? I dare say she may have spent her time in
other pursuits if she hadn't been asked (commanded would be a
better word for it) by her confessor to put down some of the
extraordinary things that had happened to her. She says in her
Life (Chap. x, 7), "Only those who are commanding me to write
know that I am writing and they are not here right now, and
almost stealing the time with difficulty, it keeps me from spin-
ning, for being in such a poor house [I have] plenty of work."
So her primary reason for writing is *obedience* to her confessors
to give an account of her spiritual progress. Later it was suggested that she guide her spiritual daughters by means of putting
into writing some of her thoughts.

As I already said, the first complete work St. Teresa composed was her autobiography or her *Life*. This was begun in
1562, the year she inaugurated the reform with the foundation
of the convent of San Jose in Avila. But before that, in 1560,

she had written what is known as her *First Spiritual Relation*, at the command of her confessor—the Dominican P. Pedro Ibañez. This spiritual relation describes what her confessor wanted to know—her method of prayer—mainly because he was interested in finding out why she was having extraordinary things happening to her. After reading this spiritual relation, P. Ibañez asked St. Teresa to write a more detailed account of her life. It seems that the founding of her convent caused a lot of commotion; to tell the whole story, another confessor, P. Garcia de Toleda (also a Dominican) asked her to enlarge the first version. The manuscript was submitted to P. Domingo Bañez, the theologian, and to the Inquisition—they kept it for many years. St. Teresa speaks of these things in her book of the *Foundations*. At about the same time, she wrote what is now the *Second Spiritual Relation*, also for Fr. Ibañez, while staying with her friend, Doña Luisa de la Cerda, in Toledo. And nine months later, she wrote her *Third Spiritual Relation* from San Jose, Avila. This was probably for her confessor Garcia de Toledo. These deal with her methods of prayer and the state of her soul. All the rest of the spiritual relations (which are brief) were written at later dates. So we can see St. Teresa did not compose her *Life* as a planned treatise. She probably began it in 1562, but did not finish it until 1565, after laying down her pen for two years.

Briefly, the *Life* is autobiographical from Chapters I to X; there is a parenthetical section of 16 chapters in which she describes the contemplative life under the figure of the Four Waters. And then she completes the book, from Chapter 28 with 12 more chapters of autobiography to Chapter 40.

The second major work, the *Way of Perfection*, was written shortly after she finished her *Life*. She says in her *Way of Perfection:* "A few days ago, they commanded me to write a true account of my life, where I also treated of some matters of prayer. It may be that my confessor will not wish you to see it. For this reason I shall put down here some of the things which were going to be said there and other things that I may deem necessary" (Prologue, 4). So the work was written primarily for the edification of her nuns. Some interpret the date as 1563; others, 1566, according to whether she means she finished or started writing her *Life*. 1566 seems more exact since she already knew what was in the *Life*, and her confessors thought it was too intimate to put into the hands of her sisters.

The *Way of Perfection* has for its goal: to teach her daughters to love prayer. She discusses such things as observance of the Rule, mutual love, humility and all the other Christian virtues. It is in this book she uses the famous simile of the game of chess. She also brings up some interesting theological problems —for instance, whether a soul in sin can experience contemplation. And, finally, it is in this book she gives her lengthy exposition of the Our Father. It is perhaps the most practical of her books for those who are interested in learning to live a spiritual life.

She wrote this work twice and she called it the *Pater noster.* The second edition is a corrected edition and a more polished one. This is the one found in the Carmel of Valladolid, and the one submitted to her first editor, Fray Luis de Leon. This second version was written in 1569. In the same year, she wrote her *Exclamations of the Soul to God,* or, as the 1588 edition of Fray Luis de Leon calls it, *exclamacions o meditaciones del alma a su Dios.* These are brief out-pourings which St. Teresa composed after receiving communion. There are no original manuscripts of it.

We know when St. Teresa started writing the book of *Foundations* because she tells us in the prologue of the same book: "while staying in San Jose in Avila in the year 1562, which was the same year that this monastery was founded, I was commanded by Father Garcia de Toledo, the Dominican who at the time was my confessor to write about the foundations of that monastery with many other things, that whomever may read it, if it is published, will see. Now while staying in Salamanca in the year 1573, which is eleven years later, I confessed to a Father Rector of the company, called Master Ripalda who having seen this book of the first foundation thought it would be a service to Our Lord to write about the other seven monasteries which had been founded after this one through the goodness of Our Lord, together with the beginning of the monasteries of the Discalced Fathers of this first Order; and so he has commanded me to do it." We see by this that Teresa began her work, but it is obvious she did not complete it until the last foundation was made. She wrote some chapters in 1574, others in 1576, and finished the work the year she died, in 1582.

St. Teresa gave the book no title. From the work we get the best glimpse of St. Teresa through the things she did and the anecdotes she tells. It is the work I would recommend to be read first to a person who might be interested in reading the works of St. Teresa. It helps to put her into historical perspective. Since it is practically pure narrative, it is easy reading.

The last and greatest of St. Teresa's major works, the *Interior Castle*, was written in 1577 while St. Teresa was happily kept in her convent of Toledo by order of her major superiors. She and Gracian were talking of some spiritual matters, and St. Teresa remembered how she had written it in her *Life*, which was in the hands of the Inquisition. It was then suggested she try to recall it and put it into writing. Thus, in a more leisurely atmosphere than she was accustomed to, St. Teresa composed, with a little more order, a treatise on the soul in the state of grace. As she states in the preface, she began the work on Trinity Sunday, June 2, 1577. She completed it at Avila on November 9th of 1577. But she states in the fifth mansions that almost five months had gone by since she began. So she spent six weeks writing the first five chapters, and another six weeks finishing the other two and one-half chapters.

This work is the most logical of her works and perhaps the most important work of mystical literature ever composed, outside of the *Living Flame of Love* by St. John of the Cross. As we mentioned, St. Teresa's simile is a large castle made of a single diamond, or of clear crystal (today, a glass house) in which there are many mansions with many rooms—and, like a medieval town, the King's court is located in the very center. She describes the various stages of a soul striving to reach this King. The Mansions can be briefly described under these simplified titles: state of grace; practice of prayer; exemplary life; prayer of quiet; spiritual betrothal; prayer of union; and spiritual marriage.

Very close in affinity to the *Interior Castle* is the book, *Conceptions of the Love of God*, or, as it is sometimes entitled in Spanish, *Conceptos del amor de Dios escritos por la Beata Madre Teresa de Jesus sobre algunos palabras de los Cantares de Salomon*. For this reason, it is called more simply in Spanish, *Meditaciones sobre los cantares*. She wrote it for her daughters between 1571 and 1573, probably at Avila, again at her confessor's command. It was a dangerous although popular theme to use for mystical writers of her day. We have only to recall the *Spiritual Canticle* of St. John. Fray Luis de Leon spent five years in prison for daring to translate the *Canticle of Canticles* into the vernacular. So it is not surprising that he did not include this work in his edition of the works in 1588. It first appeared in print in 1611 under the editorship of Gracian. Like St. John's work, it compares the soul to the bride in the *Canticle* and the false kinds of peace she is likely to encounter in her search for the bridegroom.

The remaining minor works can be put under two headings —legal writings and collected notes. In founding a convent St. Teresa was required to draw up statutes and ordinances for the governing of her nuns and instructions for a visitation to be made, to make it easier for the Father visitor. St. Teresa did not write her constitutions until around 1567. It seems her daughters were content to follow her verbal instructions until then. Father General gave them his approval during a visit to Avila, and they were followed very closely until this time of renewal by many convents of nuns. They are a sort of commentary on the Rule—a more detailed interpretation of the way of life prescribed by the Rule.

The *Visitation of Convents* actually turns out to be more of an exhortation to the sisters than an aid to the Father visitator, on how they should act toward one another, rather than toward him. It is believed to have been written in 1576. It was primarily for Fr. Gracian, provincial, whom St. Teresa thought was a little too expansive and frank and a little too credulous, when visiting her communities of nuns.

The difference between the two works entitled (in English) *Maxims* is that the *Avisos* to her nuns were probably devout sayings collected by her daughters and compiled, and the others, called in Spanish, *Apuntaciones* (or *Notes)*, were found in her breviary when she died. The dates of composition are unknown. But her *Maxims* appeared along with the *Way of Perfection* in 1583.

The *Spiritual Challenge* derives from a custom among the Carmelites to challenge each other to perform religious practices so as to give some further motive for leading a holy life. The prioress would have written an answer to this spiritual challenge which is believed to have come from the friars at Pastrana.

The Judgment (given by St. Teresa) *upon Various Writings on the Words, "Seek thyself in Me,"* is a treatise in which she writes a judgment on commentaries written by four people on the words, "Seek thyself in Me," which she is supposed to have heard in a vision and communicated to her brother Lorenzo de Cepeda. The Bishop of Avila was supposed to have judged the commentaries, but he shrewdly sent them to St. Teresa herself. This was in 1576.

The only commentary I wish to make on these writings now, is that it helps one to know why they were written and when, because it has some bearing on St. Teresa's doctrine—she grew and changed her opinion, so we cannot judge all her writings as if each were the last word. But we can appreciate her lively personality in every word she wrote—and what she said is as applicable today as when it was written. Her expressions sometimes may be dated, but her message is timeless.

St. Teresa's Bookmark

Neither disturbed

Nor frightened be.

Everything changes;

Only God remains

the same.

Patience

Is all we need.

One lacks nothing

Who has God;

He is plenty.

St. Teresa loved to compose little poems (and some not so little) called *coplas, romances* and *villancicos* (couplets, ballads carols) for special feast days, or to entertain her sisters. Many of these were spontaneous, and quite good according to her well traveled chaplain, Julian de Avila.

Her famous *Bookmark* is different in that it does not rhyme. But it has its own internal rhyme. It was found in her Breviary after she died at Alba. Fr. Gracian, aware of the importance of her writings, signed the back of the bookmark attesting to its authenticity.

St. Teresa's Style

"For the love of God, let me work at my spinning-wheel and go to choir and perform the duties of the religious life like the other sisters. I am not meant to write. I have neither the health nor the intelligence for it" (quoted by Peers, vol I, xxxix from P. Gracian, *Lucidario del verdadero espiritu*, chap. V).

This is what St. Teresa thought of her avocation to write, a task which was imposed upon her by her confessors. It is one of the ironies of history that she is included in every anthology of Spanish literature, and is more admired by her Spanish audience than Charlotte Bronte is by the English-speaking world. It was her total lack of effort to be a literary figure that has put her forever among the great writers, not only of Spanish prose, but of prose in any language. She has influenced people as different as Henry Wallace and the great prose writer, Ernest Hemingway. She has changed people's lives entirely through her writings— people like Edith Stein, who was so taken by her sincerity and honesty that she adopted not only her faith but her vocation as a Carmelite.

Some authorities have called her no writer at all. Menéndez Pidal, the Spanish literary critic, has said that St. Teresa can hardly be said to write at all—she talks in writing. And if that is the criterion of good writing, then she succeeds in being a good writer. The foremost authority on the Spanish language of St. Teresa's day—and it has only been since that time that the language attained the unified status it was to have—namely, the great humanist, Juan de Valdés, says in his work on Spanish philology called *Diálogo de la lengua*, "to tell the truth I observe very few things of style because the style I have is natural to me and without any affectation whatever, I write as I speak" (Del Rio, I, p. 290).

We may logically ask then, what was the language St. Teresa spoke. To say it was Spanish is to oversimplify the question. Most people do not realize what a unique position St. Teresa occupies in developing her own language. As Del Rio says in his

History of the Spanish Language, speaking of her work the *Life*, "This extraordinary autobiography opens new furrows in profane literature as well as in religious literature" (vol. I, p. 190).

The 16th century saw not only the political unification of Spain but the unification of its language as well. Castilian, which was the predominate language of the Iberian Peninsula, was in full evolution phonetically. This accounts for the diverse pronunciations of Spanish in the New World. It was only at the close of the 15th century that Castilian was regarded as a language capable of being taught and capable of having a grammar. Castilian derived from Latin and Latin was still the language of the learned.   French and Italian also had its influence through Italianized poets like Garcilaso de la Vega, Boscan and Juan de Mena, who all had studies outside of Spain. After the popular art of Romanceros and Cancioneros (then in vogue as literary devices) attracted attention to the spoken language through ballads, and after the people, through the conquest of the Americas, began to awaken to a national consciousness, Spanish began to come into its own. Thus Juan de Valdés, in writing his *Diálogo de la lengua* in 1533 was courageously proclaiming that the standard for Castilian was not the literary italianized or latinized modes of speech then also in vogue, but rather the spoken tongue—the language of every-day usage.   Even so, among the purists, the vulgar tongue was considered unworthy and unfitted to express more lofty ideas. Castilian was used in works only for the unlearned. This helps to understand St. Teresa's insistence that she was unlearned in writing; it helps us to understand why she turned away the novice who came with her Latin bible.

The Castilian spoken by the people of Avila was perhaps among the best dialects of the language. It was somewhat rough in the mouths of the peasants and more refined in the mouth of the genteel class to which St. Teresa belonged.   Today, the Castilian looks down his nose at the softer, slower, sweeter and more musical speech of the Andalusian or of the South American.   His speech is more brusque and raspy, gutural. However, there is evidence that St. Teresa's speech was perhaps closer to the pronunciation of the Andalusian than to the Castilian of today, but more precise in pronunciation than the Andalusian of today.

St. Teresa spelled phonetically because there was no standard to go by in this evolving tongue. Thus her pronunciation comes through in her writing, and it is a valuable witness to the pronunciation of Castilian in the 16th century. Her Spanish is correct but colloquial and sometimes misspelled. She wrote with haste—*a vuela pluma* (pen a'flying), she says—and, as she also says, without revision, so that we have the spoken tongue as no other writer has been able to capture it without a tape recorder.

By far the most important work from this point of view, is her *Life*. This was her first work, she is least self-conscious and most natural. It contains more colloquialisms, more refrains and popular proverbs than the other works. It is full of common figures of speech, which one uses unconsciously in his speech. Even today, popular sayings, proverbs and platitudes are part of the speech of the people—even more so in Spanish than in English.

There is nothing of the *litérateur* about her. However, in later works, she is seen correcting some of her more obvious mistakes and polishing up a phrase or two. It is interesting to know that she wrote her *Interior Castle* in Toledo. Perhaps the combination of place and companions produced a more studied and less colloquial work which the *Interior Castle* is. Toledo was supposed to be the center of learning, and the language spoken there was considered the purest Castilian since the reign of Alfonzo X, the great patron of the arts. And it was here that St. Teresa spent some time before with her friend, Doña Luisa de la Cerda.

Her style was recognized by the best, even in her day. The learned editor, Fray Luis de Leon, changed very little when he compiled her works. He says: "It was a gross error to wish to correct certain words, for if one understood Castilian well, one would see that the Madre's is elegance itself—I doubt if there be any work in our language to equal hers in the art of graceful expression, purity, ease of style, grace and manipulation of words and a certain general air of elegant ease" (quoted from Hoorneavt, *St. Teresa in her writings*, p. 190).

In the prologue of her *Foundations*, St. Teresa says: "I believe that many very important things will be left out and others which one could do without, will be said . . ." Well, she is not entirely wrong in this statement, because, just as in conversation ideas sometimes come faster than the tongue can deliver them, and sometimes a gesture will take the place of a word or an inflection of the voice will save many words, this is how St. Teresa transposed her speech into writing. This at times makes for difficult reading and impossible translation, but the context usually supplies the sense. For instance, she says in the *Life* (xxviii, 6): "Difficult things drive me to devotion and the more, the more" *(me hacen devocion las cosas difficultosas y mientras mas, mas)*, meaning the more difficulties there are, the more is the devotion they arouse in me. This ellipsis is one of the characteristics of her writing.

Another is her remarkable use of repetition—which ordinarily is a speech device rather than a written one. These are used mainly to show emphasis. Some examples are these taken from her works:

> *De nosotros no podemos en nada, nada . . .* (Life xx, 7).
> (Of ourselves we can do nothing, nothing . . .)

> *Oh hermanas . . . acostumbraos, acostumbraos . . .* (Way of
>   Perfection, xxvi, 2)
> (Oh, sisters, accustom yourselves, accustom yourselves . . .)

And she even repeats as much as three times in this sentence, speaking of her unworthiness before the Lord. "Qué de ello, qué de ello, qué de ello y otras mil veces lo puedo decir, me falta para esto." (How far, how far, how far and a thousand times over I can say it, am I from this (Life, xxxix, 6).

St. Teresa plays with words, not only by repetition, but also by sound or alliteration. Here is an example of both taken from her *Life: En estos tiempos de quietud dejas descansar el alma con su descanso"* (Life XV, 8). (In these times of quiet, let the soul rest in its rest.) It loses everything in translation.

Another example (and there are many) can be found in her *Interior Castle* where she is asking if the sinner can leave this palace to sin. *"Por ventura puede el pecador para hacer sus maldades, apartarse de este palacio"* (Mansions VI, 10).

One explanation of her use of alliteration is that she liked jingles and she had a sense of rhythm, and this is not relegated to her more polished works, either. There are plenty of examples in her *Life*.

The best example of her conversational style is her use of long, involved sentences when she is explaining something seriously, like prayer. They are filled with parenthetical remarks and so involved does she become in her sentence that by the time she is finished, she has almost lost the original sense of it.

Here is a long sentence from the 23rd chapter of her *Life*, vs. 12, where she is speaking of the book, *The Ascent of Mount Sion*, by Bernardino de Laredo: "Looking through books to see if I could learn how to explain the prayer I was preaching, I found in one called the *Ascent of the Mount*, which treated of the union of the soul with God, all the signs I had in that prayer of not thinking of anything when I was in that prayer, and I marked the parts with lines and gave the book to him so that he and the other cleric I have mentioned, a holy servant of God, might look at it and tell me what I should do, and if they thought I should leave aside prayer altogether, for why did I have to meddle in these dangers, for at the end of almost 20 years I had to make prayer, I had not come out ahead except for the deceits of the devil, it would be better not to make it, although this also would make it hard for me to bear, because I had already sampled how my soul was without prayer."

But these long sentences are interspersed with equally short ones, as one does in conversation. These short, lively sentences are found in abundance in her *Way of Perfection*, as well as in the *Interior Castle*, where she is explaining to her daughters the road to prayer. "Let us force ourselves my sisters for love of the Lord. Let us leave our fears and reason in his hands. Let us forget this natural frailty which can take possession of us. The care of these bodies, let the prelates have it. Let them reconcile that. Our is only to travel quickly to see this Lord" (Interior Castle III, 2, 8).

She asks questions and answers them, "What then is this? Where does it come from? I will tell you . . ." (Castle V, 2,11). And also interspersed among her works are apostrophes or exclamations, like: "Good heavens! Oh my God! O Supreme Good! O my Rest! O Lord of my soul!" And her most frequent one: "*Valga me Dios!*" *God help me!* She even says, "*Maldita sea!*" Damn it!—which is hardly ever translated that way!

But more important than her sentence structure is her use of vocabulary and her images. The key to her vocabulary is naturalness, simplicity and without affectation—a thing she warned her daughters against. In her book, *Method for the Visitation of Convents*, 42, she says to her nuns: "Prefer to use

the plain words rather than the odd in these cases." She practiced what she preached, for she uses no technical terms, no
latinisms nor Italian constructions. She doesn't even use the
right terms for mystical theology, and when she does, she mis-
spells them. Her misspellings, as I said, give us an idea of how
she spoke; for instance, when she spells *religion, relision,* or
iglesia as *ilesia,* it means her pronunciation was more dental than
velar or gutteral, as many Castilians speak today.

She prefers words of a popular origin, like *hablas* in place
of *locuciones; talks* instead of *locutions.* She borrows terms
from other writers: it is probable she took her terms "prayer of
recollection" and "prayer of quiet" from Osuna, whose book
Third Spiritual Alphabet influenced her. And never is her popular speech more evident in her use of diminuatives. These are
formed by the addition of various endings in Spanish, like *ico,*
illo, ito, uelo. They can mean smallness, but also affection,
condescension and even disgust. We have something like this in
English. *Mariposita* for *mariposa; palomita* for *paloma; pastor-
cito* for *pastor; cosita* for *cosas* (trifles); *gusanillo* for *gusano;*
even things like *consideraciones,* she says *nuestras consideracion-
cillas,* meaning our poor little meditations. This usage of
diminuatives is very colloquial and frowned upon by purists of
the written language.

Finally, her whole vocabulary of images gives us not only a
glimpse of her likes and dislikes but her interests and her background as well. It is not at all surprising to a woman whose
brothers were soldiers in the army of the conquest in the new
world—one of whom died in battle on the fields of Quito,
Ecuador—to think of life in terms of a warfare, especially the
religious life. Thus, her writings are full of military figures. She
is a true product of the humanist renaissance, whose ideal was
the rugged individualist. "Be strong men," she counselled her
daughters. "If they do what is in themselves, the Lord will make
them so manly they will frighten men" (Way VII, 8). "Fight
like strong men even to dying in the endeavor" (Way XX, 2).

She passes from one figure to another—always into a battle.
She is talking about the solitary bird—"Here is the pain of having
to come back to life. Here it sprouted wings to fly well; now the
bad feathers have fallen," then without any warning she says,
"Here now is raised from it all the banner for Christ . . . the
governor of this fortress mounts the highest tower" (Life XX,

22). Into the fray she goes!

Sometimes she realizes this as, for instance, when she is talking about a garden and suddenly finds herself in the battle again. She says (Life XX, 23) "Behold the gardener made governor of the fortress." This is what makes her so lovable; she is able to poke fun at her own foibles.

I think everyone knows that St. Teresa was partial to water —it fascinated her in any form. She drew many famous similes from it, the most famous of which is found in her *Life*. She explains the different kinds of prayer by the way one obtains water. She says: ". . . I don't find a more appropriate thing to explain some things of the Spirit than that of water; and it's because, since I know so little and my wits don't help and I am so fond of this element, I have looked at it with more attention than other things" (Castle, IV, 2).

This has been the perennial problem of the mystic—to translate his experience into words or concepts. This very problem has given us some of the most sensual literature ever published; it has given us ironically some of the most material writings and some of the most vivid images conceived. Thus St. Teresa says in her *Life*: ". . . but this language of the spirit is so difficult to explain to those without learning, like myself, that I will have to look for some way to explain it and it may be fewer times that I succeed in finding a good comparison" (Life XI, 6). "I did nothing except draw comparisons to make myself understood" (Life XXVII, 3).

In these comparisons she speaks of small animals, and insects (as the metaphor of the silkworm in the 5th mansions of the *Interior Castle)*, of ants, bees, birds, butterflies, caterpillars, cobwebs, doves, eagles, flies, hens, lizards, moths, snakes, sparrows, spiders, toads, tortoises, turtle doves and worms. Of large animals, she mentions donkeys, dragons, horses, lambs, lions and sheep. The only flowers she mentions are carnations, roses, rosemary and thistles. In the case of rosemary, she is interested only in its dry sticks, and only in the thorns of the thistle. The figures she used most, outside that of water, are the *way*, *fire*, *light*, *sunlight*. For instance, the humanity of Christ is always described in terms of whiteness and light. And a thing of special importance today in our Resurrectional theology—she almost always saw him as risen from the dead (Castle XXIX) *(siempre la carne glorificada) (Hoornaert p. 295).*

The book with the fewest illustrations is, naturally, the *Foundations*—it is mostly narrative. The *Spiritual Relations* also are lacking in illustrations. The *Life* has many figures but the *Way of Perfection* has more. Then comes the *Conceptions of the love of God*, and finally, the *Interior Castle*, the most mystical of them all.

In conclusion, I would like to point out that the writings of St. Teresa are not only mystical treatises that can be of some benefit to your spiritual life, they can also be enjoyable to read, and when you read her writings, it may be of some comfort to know you are not just reading pious literature, but you are reading some of the masterpieces of Spanish literature, and a mystical literature that holds its own in any religion

Note: I have drawn heavily for my examples in this chapter on the works of E. Allison Peers: *St. Teresa of Jesus and other Essays and Addresses.* (London: Faber and Faber, 1953), and R. Hoornaert: *St. Teresa in Her Writings.* (New York, Benziger Bros., 1931). Peers read both Hoornaert and R. Menendez Pidal, Moguel and Hatzfeld who wrote on St. Teresa's style. I also have consulted them.

St. Teresa's Castle

In this chapter I would like to discuss some of St. Teresa's basic concepts in the *Interior Castle*, so that when you read it, you will have a clearer idea of her thought. As I stated before, she was commanded to write it. But how she came to write it has an interesting background. We could say we owe it to the Inquisition! It seems that Father Gracian, her Provincial, and St. Teresa were one day talking of spiritual matters when she made the chance remark, "Oh, how well I made that point in the book of my *Life* (referring to her autobiography) which is at the Inquisition." Fr. Gracian, not to be deterred by the Holy Office, said in answer, "since we can't get at that, why not recall what you can of it, and write a fresh book and expound the teaching in a general way, without saying to whom the things that you describe have happened" (P. Gracian in Ribera's biography of St. Teresa; quoted from Peers works, vol. II, p. 188). He also referred Teresa to her confessor, whom he knew she wouldn't disobey.

Another day, due to a snow storm, she found herself detained at an inn on the high Castilian plain. It was at this time she confided in an old friend—a Jeronymite Friar, Diego de Yepes—how she was inspired to begin the book. Diego de Yepes told this to Teresa's first publisher, Luis de Leon, years later after her death: "On the eve of the festival of the Most Holy Trinity, she was thinking about what subject she should chose for the treatise, when God, who disposes all things in due form and order, granted this desire of hers, and gave her a subject. He showed her a most beautiful crystal globe, made in the shape of a castle and containing seven mansions, in the seventh and innermost of which was the King of Glory, in the greatest splendor, illuminating and beautifying them all" (letter of Fray Diego de Yepes to Fray Luis de Leon from P. Silverio Obras II, 490: quoted from Peers Works Vol. II, p. 187).

Whether she meant this in a miraculous way, we don't know, but there is no doubt that St. Teresa was influenced by the Gospel of St. John (14:2), for she says in her first chapter, ". . . which is to consider our soul as a castle all of diamond or very clear crystal where there are many rooms just as in heaven there are many mansions" (Mansions I, 1, 1).

This conception of the soul as a place wherein dwells the Lord is common among spiritual writers. St. Teresa has already used the image of the fortress twice in her autobiography (chap. 18, 4 and chap. 20,22) and in the *Way of Perfection* she refers to a walled city, and a place where we may withdraw behind closed doors (chap. 3, 2 and chap. 28, 6).

The writings of two of her favorite authors made reference to walled castles very similar to her concept: In the *Third Spiritual Alphabet* by Francisco de Osuna (chap. 4, 2 & 3) he speaks at length of the necessity of guarding one's soul from the assaults of its enemies, the world, the flesh and the devil and he likens this to the methods of defending a fortified castle. Bernardino de Laredo in his book, *The Ascent of Mount Sion* speaks of building the new Jerusalem of crystal and precious stones, setting up its walls and towers on the level plain, which is the Christian soul (chap. 2, 46).

Aside from her reading, the physical aspect around St. Teresa would be reason enough for her to use the symbol of the castle for the soul. "Castles in Spain" are legendary throughout the world. And St. Teresa lived in a walled city—that of Avila surrounded by medieval fortifications. The well-known Spanish author, Miquel de Unamuno was convinced that "the castle of the *Mansions* is the city of Avila."

There are writers on the Carmelite Saints who see in St. Teresa's imagery, the possible influence of St. John of the Cross. A castle in the middle of the city of Medina del Campo, where St. John lived seems to fit the description of St. Teresa's castle, aside from the fact that hers was of diamond or clear crystal. Without making more of an issue over any particular castle which might have inspired St. Teresa (if there was one) in the writings of St. John of the Cross, there is also mention of castles. This and other similarities of expression have led these same writers to conclude that there was certainly a mutual influence between St. Teresa and St. John of the Cross. St. Teresa's advanced experience in mystical matters and St. John's advanced theological knowledge of such things helped them both to put forth their doctrine in a more precise form. Thus the concept of the soul as a castle is an image they shared.

St. John alludes to the word *mansions* three times in his works. The first time in the *Ascent of Mount Carmel* (bk. II, c. 11, 9) he says that those who faithfully respond to divine grace will progress from stage to stage, and that there are seven mansions, which are the gradations of love leading to the wine-cellar of perfect charity. St. Teresa also uses and comments upon the same passage from the *Song of Songs* (2,4). "The king brought me into the wine-cellar and conferred upon me his love."

In the second reference to mansions, also from the *Ascent* (II, 11, 11) St. John refers to these seven mansions as *aposentos* (rooms), which is the same word she used for the divisions of her mansions in her opening chapter of the *Interior Castle*.

In the third mention of the mansions, St. John is commenting on the biblical text from St. John's gospel, "In my Father's house there are many mansions," and he tells us that these should be understood as the stages of spiritual progress. This comes from the *Living Flame* (1,2). There is an interesting difference between the terminology of the two saints. Whereas St. John uses the latinized word *mansiones*, St. Teresa, as was her style, sticks to the more vernacular word *moradas*. They can mean the same thing, as I pointed out in the Introduction.

Over and above the similarity of terminology of the two saints, their mutual influence becomes more apparent in their approach. St. John's greatest contribution to mystical literature is not in his enumeration of stages of progress or his approach to prayer, which follow a long Christian tradition, but rather it is emphasis on the crises of the transitions which one falls into in his practice of prayer. How to take advantage of these crises —these different phases, in order to progress is the reason he writes. In no other work does St. Teresa so closely imitate this same approach. She says in the Prologue of the *Mansions*, ". . . as the news of these monasteries of Our Lady of Carmel need someone to clear up for them some doubts about prayer and (what appeared to him) women better understand their own language and with the love they have for me, it would make them pay more attention to what I might say." The words in parenthesis refer to Fr. Gracian.

Practically all the commentators who followed St. John and St. Teresa, have tried to make them fit into the traditional three-fold way of the spiritual life, namely, the purgative, the illuminative and the unitive way. They did not digress from these basic categories, but it is not apparent that they wrote with these divisions in mind. Certain existentialists today look upon the three-fold way as if it were optional. For instance, some would rather begin with illumination, etc. Who wouldn't? But the three-fold way merely enumerates the stages of growth which are based on human nature. The purifications of St. John of the Cross are laid down in stages, and in the *Interior Castle* St. Teresa has one pass successively through the rooms of each mansion—sometimes quickly, other times slowly. The two saints have devised this quest for God as a love relationship which either grows or dies.

Neither must we look upon St. Teresa's divisions as limiting our freedom or confining our expression. She is personalistic in so far as she allows us to wander about the Castle, or even to come back out of it, and she allows us any number of ways to enter it. She says in the First Mansion (2,12), "For this reason do I say you should not think of a few rooms but a million because in many ways do souls enter here, one and all with good intentions." She does not want to leave us with the impression that one room is automatically linked together with another (Mansions I, 2,3). Following the image of a medieval town, there was usually a jumble of dwellings lying in concentric circles, separated by defensive walls until one reached the innermost castle with its chapel. This would fit St. Teresa's description. She speaks of the mansions in the plural. In speaking of the Seventh Mansion, now in the singular, some authors see the influence of St. John of the Cross. She locates this mansion *en el centro y mitad de todas estas* (in the center and middle of all the others). It is here that the King, the Beloved, the Holy Trinity dwells.

It is unusual for St. Teresa to use this term *centro* (center) in referring to the soul, because it is academic and abstract. On the other hand, St. John follows the terminology of the earlier German mystics. These were at the time available in Latin. He not only uses the term, but goes to great lengths to explain it, implying that God is at the center of our Being. In our own age Paul Tillich popularized a concept of God, taken from Eastern religious terminology as "the ground of our being." According to these two mystics, it is at the center of the soul that one finds God. It is here that the self-knowledge which St. Teresa wants us to cultivate, is completely gained. They teach us that one does not find oneself" and then afterward seek God. Rather-er it is in seeking him that one finds oneself.

Let us complete St. Teresa's analogy. First of all, the castle in its entirety is the soul. We all have many mansions to dwell in, and we are all capable, potentially, of reaching what she terms the Seventh Mansion. It is not a case of God coming to us. He already dwells in the innermost center of this Seventh Mansion. It is a case of our going within to dwell with him. Moreover, she says, "It will be a consolation for you to delight in this interior castle . . . you can enter and walk around it at any hour" (Mansions, Epilogue, 1). No permission was needed, as it was for going to the chapel to pray. So St. Teresa approaches the subject of prayer from the point of view of presence, wheth-er we kneel before the Blessed Sacrament or go before the God who dwells within us.

Even though St. Teresa recognizes many ways to enter the castle, she nevertheless has her preference. In the First Mansion (1,9) she says, "For as far as I can understand, the door for entering this castle is prayer and meditation." Once inside, she allows the greatest of freedom in the practice of prayer, because as she says, "the things of the soul always must be considered as abundant, spacious and with grandeur (Mansions I, 2,8). "This is very important for any soul that prays much or little, that it does not lay it aside or force it." This could very well be St. Teresa's commentary on both the role of women in her society and on the methods of prayer employed in her age. Women were encouraged to practice the ordinary external acts of devo-tion of the Church and were discouraged from a deeper prayer life for fear they would either end in hysteria or in some sort of Quietism. St. Teresa looked into methods of prayer through the books we have already mentioned. She found none of them satisfactory, so through her confessors and her visions she finally learned it was through friendship with Christ that she grasped what prayer was all about.

In these first Mansions St. Teresa insists on two things: the practice of self-knowledge and humility. ". . . it is a thing so important this self-knowledge that I would desire no relaxation in it, though you may ascend to the heavens" (Mansions I, 2, 9). But she also realizes that in itself, this can become an intro-spective practice, leading to feelings of great insecurity. ". . . if

we never leave our bog of miseries it is a great disadvantage."
She then gives us her method: "For this reason, I say, daughters,
let us train one's eyes on Christ—our good—and there we will
learn true humility [she also includes Our Lady in a few places]
and the intellect has to adorn itself and as I have mentioned,
self-knowledge will not make us petty and cowardly" (Mansions
I, 2, 11). An abstract approach to prayer, she has learned since
she wrote her *Life* is now far from her thoughts, that is, one that
does not take into account the Incarnation of Jesus Christ. Even
in the highest mansions she reminds us that meditation on Jesus
Christ is absolutely necessary. She says in chapter seven, vs. 14,
of her Sixth Mansion, ". . . however spiritual you may be, don't
so flee from corporeal things that it ever may appear the most
Sacred Humanity causes you harm." She had gone astray for a
period of time, but later came to realize how important the
Humanity of Jesus was, for she says, "Even when I might, I want
no good except that acquired through whom all good came to
us," (Mansions VI, 7, 15), namely Jesus Christ. (I will say more
about this later.)

I have seen and read resumes of the stages of the *Interior
Castle* in which there is no mention of Jesus Christ. So important is he to this whole process of advancement in prayer that
St. Teresa never fails to bring us back to him whenever she can.
He is so important that she does not assign any other analogical
existence to him except that as Master of the Castle, who dwells
in the innermost mansion. To depict his all-pervading influence
throughout the Castle, she makes all the stones out of glass,
crystal or diamond so that the brilliant sun of his glory will be
reflected in every corner, except when the soul is in serious sin,
and covered with pitch.

The enemies of the soul she says, dwell in the moat around
the castle; they are "snakes, vipers and poisonous creatures."
Her analogy is accurate, for it was the custom in medieval times
to deter ones enemies, not only by digging a moat and filling it
with water, but also to put venemous creatures in it. These are
the world, the flesh and the devil. She also adds an interesting
detail—that these creatures sometimes enter the castle, especially
in the first three mansions, and even up to the Seventh Mansion.
Contrary to the Illuminist doctrines taught in her day, man is
never so perfect that he cannot fall prey to sin, until he is completely united with God. The presence of these creatures within

the castle also fits her analogy. In medieval times castles were often equipped with what they called "bear gardens" of rare animals for the entertainment of the family and their guests.

It has been contended that St. Teresa shows little appreciation for the body in this work of hers. That is not a fair assessment of a treatise which is directed at the over-importance of the body to the detriment of the soul. She does include the body in her analogy. Some commentators have placed it outside the castle. This is not what she says. It forms the outwall of the castle, which makes it part of the castle. She says in the First Mansions, "all our concern is in the courseness of the setting or the wall of the castle, which are these bodies" (Mansions I, 1, 2). She not only appreciates what the body is, she appreciates its limitations, and is the first to point them out to her sisters with an understanding born of her infirmities. She says in the Sixth Mansions (chap. 7, 6), "It will also seem to some souls that they cannot think about the Passion . . . I can't imagine what they are thinking about, because for angelic spirits, separated from all corporeal things is to be always fired in love, but it is not for those who live in a mortal body." She also includes within the castle certain bodily functions such as the interior senses, among which, the most troublesome is the imagination. These, together with the faculties of the soul, the intellect and the will, are called in different places *guards*, *governors*, *butlers* and *stewards*. Used properly, they serve the spiritual progress of the soul in its quest for the innermost reaches, where the Master of the castle dwells.

Let us examine this analogy of the Master, Lord and King of the castle. Both St. Teresa and St. John of the Cross take their inspiration from the biblical *Song of Songs*, and refer to this Royal apartment of the Seventh Mansion as a wine-cellar. In the *Spiritual Canticle*, St. John comments on the stanza of his poem, *en la interior bodega* (in the inmost cellar), where he says, "We can say these stages or cellars of love are seven . . . This cellar the soul speaks of here is the last and most intimate stage of love in which the soul can place itself in this life" (Spiritual Canticle 17, 3). Although St. John's gradations are of love, they both call it "the inmost cellar."

St. Teresa uses the same image in the Fifth Mansions (1,12) where she says,". . . The Bride in the *Canticle* says: The King carried me to the wine cellar or he put me I believe it says. And it does not say she went. It also says that she was wandering about seeking her Beloved in all directions." This is reminiscent of the Bride of St. John's Canticle. St. Teresa continues, "This I understand is the cellar where the Lord wants to put us when and how he wills . . . His Majesty has to put us in the center of our soul and enter in it himself." St. Teresa is saying that to arrive at this state of perfection is outside of our own efforts. The first three mansions correspond to St. John's active nights. After entering the Fourth Mansion, it is God who does the work. Our efforts thereafter are only dispositive, although still very important if we are to progress.

In this Sixth Mansion (chap. 8, 1) she says, ". . . the farther ahead the soul advances, the more escorted it is with this good Jesus . . ." Prayer is always a love relationship with a very definite object—Jesus Christ. She carries her analogy to the extreme with a delicacy lacking even in St. John's writings. She says, "in this temple of God in this mansion of his, he alone and the soul enjoy each other in the greatest of silence (Mansions VII, 3, 11). The analogy is put in terms of Spiritual marriage, and it is the first time she uses the term, which could be the influence of St. John. The imagery is of a King who takes his bride into the hidden marriage chamber, and there they delight in the most intimate union. In this mansion it is a mixed analogy, for the wine cellar of the *Song of Songs* takes the place of the marriage chamber. But it carries with it the elements of innermost and hidden. In this union St. Teresa insists that neither the intellect nor the will are allowed to partake of this experience. It pertains to the *mas profundo centro del alma* (the deepest center of the soul) (Mansions VII, 2, 3).

St. Teresa has made up for her lost book of chivalry, supposedly written in her youth. The *Interior Castle* is in its own way a love story, a romance in the tradition of her own times. The war years were over; the Castles of Spain were no longer places of battle, but the residences of nobles and kings. The more gentle virtues were now called for. The gentle faithfulness of Oriana, who is the heroine of the much-read book *Amadis de Gaula*, the platonic love of the book *Carcel de amor*, and the polite society of the book *Doncel del mar*, are all reflected in the *Interior Castle*. Dona Teresa read all these books in her youth, and they had such an influence over the idealistic youth that at least two royal decrees forbade them—to no avail! King

Philip's decree advocated burning the books because, "they turn men's heads and especially the heads of young girls who, though prudently shut up by their mothers, spend their time with *Amadis*" (quoted by R. Hoornaert, *St. Teresa in her writings*, p. 70).

As Hoornaert says, "These books favored an extreme idealism," yet they greatly helped to refine men's minds (in spite of the royal decrees) and rendered them capable of understanding doctrines of a more elevated tone, and a more spiritual nature" (Hoornaert, p. 70). Perhaps with this background, we can appreciate what St. Teresa has written about virtue and prayer in her Castle of the soul.

PART I

THE MANSIONS

Introduction to the Interior Castle

As we have mentioned before, St. Teresa's reason for writing this book or treatise was to explain in greater detail something she had already mentioned in her autobiography, which was in the hands of the Inquisition. In her conversation with Fr. Gracian, she said, "Oh, how well I made that point in the book of my *Life*." She was evidently referring to a passage in chapter 40 of this book, which says: "Suddenly my soul was recollected and it appeared to me to be like a very bright mirror without a back nor sides nor top or bottom that wasn't all clear and in the center of it was represented to me Christ Our Lord, as I am accustomed to see him. It seemed to me in all parts of my soul I saw him clear as in a mirror . . ." (Life 50, 5). Fr. Gracian told her to write another book on the subject. After some hesitation and agony (which she describes in this introduction) she was finally inspired to write the *Interior Castle*.

She explains in this introduction that writing about these mystical matters, she can only draw on her experiences, which come from the Lord, and not on her own knowledge, which she has very little confidence in. It seems that Fr. Gracian pushed this project off on her by using the excuse that women will understand from women better than from men. Teresa is not convinced of this, and she is afraid of repetition on her part. This fear is not without some basis, because she does repeat herself occasionally, and she admits that she hadn't time to reread what she has written.

Unlike her other works, she attempts to make this book a more studied and organized work. She cleans up her colloquialisms, and organizes it into seven major headings, called "mansions." But as we read, we will see that each of these seven "mansions," always written in the plural, contain within themselves many compartments. There is another unwritten division, which is not unlike those of St. John of the Cross. It is the active and the passive aspects of prayer. The first three mansions are the active, and consider what man can do for himself, always assuming the grace of God. The other four mansions deal with what God does to the soul; they are the passive or mystical elements of prayer. She also divided prayer into three types: prayer, supernatural prayer or contemplation, and in the Fifth, Sixth and Seventh Mansions perfect contemplation. The Fourth Mansion seems to be the dividing line between the active and the passive.

In the original manuscript, there are found many erasures and additions; this shows us that St. Teresa took more care in her writing of this work. However, one of her first publishers preferred her first version of what she had written. The erasure was sloppily done, and could be deciphered. So what we have in most translations is St. Teresa's original writing.

First Mansions:
A Crystal Castle Beyond the Moat

It is here that St. Teresa describes the soul as a castle made all of crystal or diamond, so that light shines throughout, a light which emanates not from the outside, but from its very center; the closer one approaches the center, the more brilliant the light. This is how she describes the indwelling of the Blessed Trinity. She does not use the word Blessed Trinity, but the King or His Majesty, which is a more proper way to describe the Lord of the castle. And in the castle we will meet many of the Lord's servants, who direct us towards the throne room, where the King resides.

The exterior of this castle has a wall, and a moat. The exterior wall is the body. St. Teresa complains that too many people are content to view no further than the exterior wall. We think we know ourselves and other people, when we consider only our bodies. Today this is more true than ever, when we consider how much time we spend on our bodies. How many thousands of dollars go to beauty salons and physical fitness parlors! A good image is all important, and St. Teresa is saying that a good image is precisely that—an image. Our real selves are within. We deal mostly with our emotions and our imaginations —men with their strength; our appetites, desires and entertainments—all of which belong to the faculties of the body. In our relations with other people, we concentrate on good feelings toward one another; our conversations are meant never to offend, and we think we have a Christian community when we have a consensus not of belief, but of feeling. It is possible to go through life without stepping foot into the castle. And where does one find the door of the castle? St. Teresa tells us: "As far as I can understand, the door for entering into this castle is prayer and meditation" (Mansions I, 1, 7).

Knowing where the door is and entering it are two separate things. She acknowledges that there are people who, because of their total absorption in the business of this world, find it all but impossible to enter, and worse still, they become like the

34

animals in the moat around the castle, that is, engaged in sin. There are some who are able to enter, but let in the vermin with them, so that they proceed no further or even go out again. There are those who want it both ways; they pray for a time, but fall back into sin.

St. Teresa clarifies what she means by "prayer and reflection." She is not distinguishing between mental and vocal prayer she is saying that prayer without thoughts or reflection is not prayer.

In the second chapter of this First Mansion, St. Teresa digresses into a consideration of the horror of mortal sin, which she sees not only as a great deterrent to prayer, but also what it does to the soul. We know from our catechism that it casts out supernatural grace, and in this state a man cannot merit. St. Teresa makes it clear that sin does not cast out God from the soul. We know from theology that God is omnipresent in all his creation. In other words, where God is not present, there is nothing. I might add, this is a point that astronomers and scientists or physicists have not fully grasped, when they speak of black holes in the universe, where nothing exists, or infinite matter, negative space, or total vacuums. Where there is nothing, a scientists is out of his field, which is that of matter.

Now the presence of God can be understood in various ways. He can be present by his power, that is, he operates in all things, and they are subject to him. He can be present by means of his knowledge; whatever he knows, exists. He can be present by his essence, as the origin of all things. None of these presences are lost through sin, and man remains an image of God, according to his soul. But with sin and the rejection of grace, the soul loses its ability to know and love God on a supernatural plane. The person becomes blinded from the light in his soul, which is God.

This is precisely what St. Teresa is telling us, when she describes the effects of mortal sin on the soul. It is as if a black cloth were thrown over the crystal, or as if pitch were applied to it. It is here that she introduces the faculties of the soul as custodians, stewards and chief waiters, who are greatly disturbed, that is, they can no longer function in their proper role of escorting the soul to the King's chamber. To avoid sin St. Teresa mentions two virtues which are of extreme benefit. First, the fear of God, and secondly humility. We can see by this how backward our catechetical approach is today, where children are encouraged to be bold and feel important in God's eyes. So when they sin, they blame everybody except themselves, or they blame God for not making them better, while failing to make any effort to better themselves. Fear of God and humility go hand in hand, because they recognize the distance between the Creator and the creature. As she says, it is humility that makes us realize that we can do nothing good of ourselves. All the more reason not to cut off the principle of our goodness!

After down-grading her ability to explain these higher truths, St. Teresa makes the comment that we too often hear about all the things we must do in order to pray, but little about what God does to the soul. She is preparing her listeners for the fruits of her inspiration. This is also, perhaps, a commentary on the kind of books that abounded in her day. And I might add, this same kind of book abounds today, only it is worse. At least in her day they stressed the virtues, now we have a proliferation of psychology and experience.

She encourages the person to progress to other rooms of the castle, but first she wishes us to spend some time in the room of self-knowledge. We might ask ourselves just what does she mean by self-knowledge? She ties self-knowledge in with humility, and her purpose seems for us to be able to get free from ourselves and not follow human convention. Today many are engaged in encounter groups to get in touch with their feelings. We take psychological profiles, and other tests to determine what our predominate emotions are, or personality type. There are many books on the enneagram system of personality types. Is this what St. Teresa means by self-knowledge? I would say it is the exact opposite, because if she wants us to make any comparisons, it is between ourselves and God. She says, finally, ". . . that we should put our eyes on Christ our good, and on his saints and there we shall learn true humility and the intellect will have to be enriched" (Mansions I, 2, 11). She tells us that the devil plays tricks on us in these first rooms, because many are "still absorbed in the world and engulfed in its pleasures and sillyness, with its honors and pretensions," that their faculties don't have the strength "that God gave them from their human nature" (Mansions I, 2, 12). What she is saying is that we belong to a fallen race, and we need the help of his Majesty, the Blessed Mother and the saints to fight for us. Today many would call this "old theology." Today's pastors would have us by-pass all intercessors, other than Christ himself, like Protestants. What a free reign we are giving the devil and his legions!

In mortal sin, one cannot see the inner light, and even in the First Mansion the light is dim because of so many impediments, which St. Teresa likens to "snakes, vipers, poisonous creatures, wild animals, and beasts." These are things that got in the door when the person entered. She follows her analogy of the castle surrounded by a moat filled with venomous creatures, which many times slipped into the castle, when the door was open. She tells us to start dumping these impediments from the start, or else they will impede any further progress to the next mansion. The impediments she identifies as "unnecessary things and concerns." In other words, with such worldly distractions it will be almost impossible to pray.

Now she turns her attention to her Sisters, who have already progressed beyond this First Mansion. Even here they are to be ever watchful lest they wander back into the "tumult." She then gives several examples of how the Sisters can be deceived by the devil. It is very interesting that she places so much emphasis on these temptations as coming from the devil. Some of today's theologians have so effectively done away with the concept of the devil, that we now blame our sins and faults on our traumatic childhood experiences, our environment, our parents, and now even the past teachings of the Church on sin! Who is more correct? St. Peter warns us that "the devil goes about like a roaring lion seeking whom he may devour." Our Lord once told us to answer "yes if we mean yes; no if we mean no, everything else is from the devil." You will find throughout St. Teresa's writings many references to the devil. It is not just a matter of dealing with a medieval mind-set. Nor is it a matter of her experiences alone; it is a matter of not recognizing the supernatural, or of not wanting to in today's Church. The devil exists, and he meddles in human affairs, and human emotions. Thus St. Teresa warns her nuns to beware of their impulses to either great zeal for perfection, which causes them to be judgemental or indiscreet zeal for great penance, which goes counter to their health or the will of those in authority. There is not too much danger in the second of these either among nuns or laymen today.

The opposite extreme is also warned against when there

are obvious faults against rules and regulations. It is only Gospel to warn one's fellowman when he goes astray. But St. Teresa is careful to point out that the warning should go to the one involved, and not to the grapevine.

So, just what is this First Mansion we have been discussing? It is the beginning state of conversion, but since this whole treatise is about prayer, we can see in these mansions both our state of perfection and our prayer-life; they are synonymous. Everyone who believes, prays. This First Mansion for St. Teresa is attained by that person who begins to take prayer seriously and begins to take definite steps to practice it in a formal fashion; in so doing one begins his journey towards knowing his own soul, and finding God within its depths.

Second Mansions:
Don't Stop Now

This second stage of prayer characterizes the person who has already begun to practice it, and is resolved to continue in spite of the difficulties it seems to present. This person is still far from being a proficient, but he is no longer content to remain in a state of sin and compromise in his spiritual life. This person experiences a first fervor, but it is mixed with occasional falls into bad habits. Because the devil wants to impede the soul, the person suddenly finds himself in a state that he judges worse than before. Things that did not seem to bother the soul before, assume an importance that they did not have in a more lax state. So the soul is caught between the delights it has experienced in its first serious encounter with the spiritual life, and the temptation of returning to its former tranquility, where what it didn't know, didn't bother it.

St. Teresa only has one chapter about this stage, because, as she says, she has written plenty about it elsewhere. She is referring to both her *Way of Perfection*, and to her *Life*, which had already been presented to the Sisters, at least in conferences if not in her finished works. In a footnote, Padre Tomas refers us to chapters 11 through 13 of her *Life*, where she deals with some of the trials of beginners. She speaks of souls that have presumably given up everything, only to find themselves holding back on some small matter. She advocates perseverence above all, and the acceptance of the Cross as the only real way to begin. But she does recognize certain times when too much force of will does us harm rather than good. We can talk today of our advances in psychology, but what more psychological advice can be added to this passage from chapter 11, 15 of the *Life?* ". . . we are so miserable that this little jailbird of a poor soul participates in the miseries of the body and the changes in the weather and the churning of body humors often make it do, without fault of its own, what it doesn't want to do, but it suffers in any case. In the meantime the more they want to force it at these times, the evil is worse and lasts longer; then use discretion to

see when it is of this kind and don't smother the poor soul"
(Life XI, 15). She then advocates another time for prayer. This
is certainly good advice.

Another admonition that she makes is, in her words, "not
to ascend to God unless he raises one up" (Life XII, 5). She is
saying the same thing that St. John of the Cross says about
passing from meditation to contemplation. Caught up in our
fervor, we may want to advance beyond our capacity. This
could be the danger of Transcendental Meditation or centering
prayer, when it is practiced before God has given us the grace to
experience him without using our ordinary faculties. She says,
"to presume not to think and suspend thought ourselves is what
I say not to do nor to leave off working with the intellect
because we will be left like cold fools and we will do neither
one thing nor the other" (Life XII, 5). She clarifies this: ". . .
when the Lord suspends the understanding and makes it stop he
gives it that which occupies it and surprises it" (Life XII, 5).

It goes without saying that instead of attempting some
kind of abstract prayer, it is beneficial throughout one's prayer-
life, especially at this time, to keep the person of Christ ever
present to oneself, to treat him as an honored guest in one's
home, that is within one's very soul. We should try to love the
Lord as we would love our best friend. But even when a sensible
devotion is missing, and we can't seem to experience this kind of
consolation, it should not disturb us. The mere act of trying to
please him is enough. Sometimes when one has great consolations, he may be tempted to think that he is better than his
neighbor.

We shouldn't care what others think; nor in this stage
should we even think about others. This may sound strange to
our ears today when we are encouraged to keep the needs of
others before us. But everything has its time and place. St.
Teresa counsels us in the beginning to think only of God and
oneself in silence and solitude and forget spiritual favors. Determination and the cross are the weapons one needs to overcome
the devil.

Above all, we must not become discouraged, even when we
fail. Our failures themselves can be a source of benefit, at least
in the way of self-knowledge. As St. Teresa says: "Can there be
a greater evil than not finding ourselves in our own home?"
(Mansions II, 1,9). Discouragement which leads us away from

our spiritual quest to engage in other more altruistic pursuits even in the apostolate is not going to enrich our personal lives. St. Teresa says: "For believe me, if we do not have and procure peace in our house, we will not find it outside" (Mansions II, 1, 9).

St. Teresa wants us to recollect ourselves not by force, but by gentleness, and the advice of others, if necessary. She attributes many of our disturbances to the devil. Our Lady of Medjugorje is saying the same thing to those whom she is encouraging to pray. She ends this chapter with an admonition to reflect on our misery, and what we owe to God, and to beg him often for his mercy. She sees prayer as an absolute necessity in coming to know oneself and coming to know the Lord, in order to know him in the hereafter. For the person who has given up prayer, the only remedy is to start again.

St. Teresa constantly refers to the beasts, wild animals, snakes and poisonous creatures in this small chapter, which have followed the soul into the second mansion. These, of course, are the difficulties and the trials, both from our past life as well as from the devil. They seem to be most abundant in this mansion. To overcome these the soul must abandon not only its bad habits, but also any bad companions and places formerly frequented. Obviously, she is not writing only to her sisters, since they presumably have already left aside their former life. She recommends conversations with people who are equally interested in the spiritual matters that the soul is pursuing. Thus do we form associations like our own, so we have someone to talk to on the same plane.

There is a time for apostolic activity for those so inclined, but we must not think that if we are not busy on some church committee, or engaged in some liturgical function, or doing social work that we are not fulfilling our Christian duties. Nor is common prayer the best way to pray. Regardless of the amount of devotion one has, if he pursues his attempt to meditate with determination, St. Teresa believes that he is well on the road. She says: "Once placed in such a high degree as to want to deal with God alone and abandon the pastimes of the world, the most is done" (Life XI, 12). Nor does one have to be a contemplative to arrive at that degree. Some of the busiest saints have had a very high state of prayer. St. John Bosco, for instance, was given extraordinary insights and revelations. And when we think of Mother Teresa today, we see not only a busy woman, but a prayerful woman. St. Teresa, herself, was hardly an inactive person; she founded 15 convents, and was often on the move.

This desire for solitude before the Lord, if not inspired by an antisocial attitude, is itself a gift of God. The temptation on the part of many is to put these desires off until retirement or for another time when one thinks he may be less occupied. Often that time never arrives. It is a holy tension that the person of prayer must live with, and not try to destroy. And the best way to deal with this is to put periods of prayer in practice. One has no problem with interrupting his schedule to visit a close friend. That is how we must look at solitude and prayer.

The desire and the determination to continue to pray is the mark of the Second Mansion.

Third Mansions:
Throwing Caution to the Wind

In the first chapter of this Mansion, St. Teresa concerns herself with the necessity of practicing the fear of the Lord and humility. It isn't easy from what she has written to determine just what this stage of prayer consists in. She speaks first of having overcome the initial battles in beginning a life of prayer, and how having reached a certain plateau, a certain security, which comes from pure determination, that is, the determination to continue and not turn back. At the same time, there is some regret that one's life up to this point has not always been so good. One now has a tendency to make up for what has been lost time. Thus the soul takes a certain delight in practicing penance, recollection, and charitable acts. But as good as these things are, St. Teresa warns us, we must not be so overconfident as to neglect the genuine fear of the Lord, that is, that fear of the Lord which got us to where we are. As Scripture tells us the "fear of the Lord is the beginning of wisdom," but having obtained some wisdom, as David and his son Solomon, we can still fall as they did without that constant reverential fear. We are fallen creatures and ever prone to evil.

This is the Mansion that most religious persons reach. Unfortunately, it is the Mansion that most religious persons remain in if they do as St. Teresa tells them not to do. They often become complacent, and "secure" in their way of life; it is no longer one of sin and neglect of the virtues, but it is where souls often draw the line between being a good Christian, and an heroic Christian. Priests and religious will attain this degree of prayer, then often fall into a mediocre routine. It is a difficult Mansion to get out of, except to fall back into a lower Mansion. If your pastor is crabby and difficult to get along with, it is many times due to his inability to progress because he does not make a further effort. And in today's Church it is easy for such a one to get lost in organization endeavors instead of putting aside a little time to pray. But if we will observe what St. Teresa says, this is not a bad stage to be in—and even one that she

considers fortunate because the conversion has taken place—as
they say, "once begun, half done."

The attitude often arises; who am I that I should expect
any more? I am lucky to have escaped the worst aspects of this
world—look at the pimps and the prostitutes, the politicians and
the crooks. We can easily fall into the publican vs. the sinner
complex. Regardless, we cannot doubt that we are all called to
a higher life. It makes no difference where we have begun.
When I consider all the "unchurched" people, especially those
around us, I cannot write them off as really bad people, or even
anti-religious. What I see is their terrible lack of self-esteem;
they don't see themselves as hypocrites in a religious service.
God's mercy and forgiveness are beyond them.

Is it humility to consider oneself worthless? Or is it,
perhaps, laziness in not attempting to offer what little we have
in the service of the Lord. St. Teresa can never be accused of
being irresolute like the children of the 60's. Determination
was high on her list of virtues, and she reminds us of what our
Lord considered a fair evaluation of our standing before the
Lord. "When you have done all you have been commanded to
do say 'we are useless servants' " (Lk:17, 10).

She begins to treat of dryness in prayer, which may occur
more often in this Mansion, and she considers it a lack of humility to ask the Lord for sensible consolations in place of this
dryness, and reminds us that it is the cross we are following.
Moreover, in dryness we will benefit by knowing ourselves better. Because in dryness we experience ourselves stripped of all
props.

In this second chapter, St. Teresa describes for us some of
the imperfections of people who have reached this Mansion.
They live good and even virtuous lives, but they have been in
this stage so long that it is hard for them to take the advice of
others. They seem to have an intellectual grasp of the cross and
suffering, yet they in times of trial, would rather blame others
in place of seeing that they are not as perfect as they think.
She contrasts this type of person with another who benefits
from his trials by attributing them to his imperfection, and
accepts the humiliation. At least this is the way I read what St.
Teresa wrote. It is not always clear what she is thinking, and
some of her allusions, like what follows, may be a gentle correc-
tion for her wealthy benefactors. Here she mentions a person

who used to be wealthy, but is now sad because she cannot donate to the poor as he used to. The person's excuse for feeling bad is not well taken according to St. Teresa. He would be better off to forego his desire to donate, and accept his lessened wealth. In other words, many times our trials are of our own making. She also seems to be speaking of people of high standing in society, when she mentions the loss of a little honor or having people think less of them in public. Many of the well-bred (as they say) in her day did live well ordered and virtuous lives. Their houses had chapels, and they attended to daily prayers almost like monks and nuns. We had even in our own country in the Victorian Age, an elite who went to great pains in portraying a correct image, and many lived very correct lives—righteous and inhibiting. And there is something to be said for such high manners and morality. But they were proud, and any dishonor certainly could not be seen in the light of Christ's passion and indignity.

At this point, St. Teresa realizes that she is addressing the wrong crowd. She shifts her subject from high-standing people to good standing nuns in habits, and declares that it is virtue not the habit which makes the nun; the control of the passions in times of trial, and humility which makes the Christian.

Now getting back to the subject, which is the person in the Third Mansion, she writes with tongue in cheek about the penance undertaken by these people. It is with great discretion and done well within reason. By our standards today, this sounds commendable, and what most spiritual directors advise. Most will warn about getting carried away, lest we damage ourselves either psychologically or physically. You would think that St. Teresa, the saint of common sense would agree with this. She says: "Love is not yet enough to exclude reason" (Mansions III, 2, 7). "But I should like us to use it in order not to content ourselves with this way of serving God." Like St. John of the Cross, she is advocating a quicker method of reaching God. And in one sense of throwing caution to the wind, in attempting to traverse these mansions until we arrive at the last one. We must forget our natural weaknesses and even our worry about health.

She makes an allusion to prelates: "The care of these bodies let the prelates have it, they settle that matter" (Mansions III, 2, 8). She had certainly experienced this constant caution of the Bishops in setting up her convents. She wants us to rely more

on the Lord and his inspiration, because, as she said, "our business doesn't lie in what relates to the body for this is the least
important" (Mansions III, 2, 8). Our Lord said the same thing
once: "the body is useless, what is needed is the spirit."

She seems to tie this in (that is, further advancement) with
humility. Her connection (at least to me) is a little tenuous. I
think she is talking about comparing our steps with those of
others, in which we must not be concerned with what they
think about us. (St. Teresa definitely writes like a woman, and
her thought processes are more intuitive rather than analogical).
In any case, without humility, we will remain in this Mansion all
our lives with our miseries. One will have occasional consolations, but not much spiritual delight.

St. Teresa warns us that she will be treating of internal
favors in the next mansion. For now it is enough for us to know
that humble souls will feel great comfort in interior favors, but
those lacking in humility will experience distaste. I have noted
this especially with regard to all the apparitions of Our Lady
today. Simple souls are attracted and benefit from such phenomena. The intellectuals and "experts" are repelled, telling us
that we have no need of private revelation and spiritual experiences. Yet they are the first ones who promote an endless array
of symbolism.

While St. Teresa recognizes that perfection consists in
greater love, justice and truth, she is not about to write off any
of the favors the Lord bestows on prayerful people. She gives as
her reason that life is hard enough, and that if by these favors a
soul can be brought to praise God, then so be it. We might ask
here, does she differ in this from the teaching of St. John of the
Cross? As you know he would have us consider everything that
is not God, at least suspect. But we are dealing with souls who
are in the Third Mansion, and even St. John allows for some
favors to those who have not reached a higher state. But in general, I would say that St. Teresa is more lenient, since the way
she was led was full of extraordinary favors—some that St. John,
as her confessor, had to curtail.

She fully recognized the danger of letting herself be led by
these favors. Thus she exhorts all of us to follow the advice of
someone who is more religious and detached then we might be
someone "who is free from the illusions of this world." It is
interesting that she suggests an unworldly advisor rather than an

educated one. As in our day, we have an abundance of "experts," but if they are not attuned to the Holy Spirit they can also mislead us. And to these unworldly advisors, even for the the layman, she wants obedience. Many times we can go in search of one who is according to our liking, rather than for our good.

At no time in this Mansion are we so secure that we cannot be deluded either by the devil, or by our pride, and she warns that under great persecution, we can easily return to the consolations of the world because as yet we have not been sufficiently tried.

There is one last thing St. Teresa discusses, and that is taking scandal from others. In this stage, a soul has a tendency to want others around them to be perfect, or at least to follow the virtues they think they are following. So she advises us to mind our own business, and leave it to God and our prayers for the improvement of others.

In reading over these chapters on the Third Mansion, we are hardpressed to know just what it is that makes it different from the other two Mansions we have already discussed. St. Teresa seems to point out more faults and imperfections, than good points. As we said in the beginning, it is here that one has taken hold of his life and decided to pursue a life of virtue and prayer. It is here that one is ready to recognize his inabilities, and imperfections, and work at doing something about them. Precluding a miraculous conversion, this is the soul that God is more likely to favor in other ways. As St. Teresa says, the Lord "grants them no small mercy because they are very near to ascending higher" (Mansions III, 2, 12).

Fourth Mansions:
Waters of Delight

This Fourth Mansion is the dividing line between our natural attempts at prayer and real supernatural prayer. At no time can we say (and St. Teresa insists on this) that one is purely from us and the other from God; God is always present even in our natural ways of acting. But there are states of prayer that come directly from God without any effort on our part. In these first two chapters of the Fourth Mansion St. Teresa attempts to distinguish the difference between them. She admits that she finds it hard to describe them adequately. She resorts to a favorite metaphor—one that she has used before in her work called the *Life*. This is the metaphor of water, which always fascinated her, and in this case the two methods of obtaining it— one through an aqueduct and the other from a spring. But we are getting ahead of our material. (The water is mentioned in the second chapter. We will come back to this.)

In the first chapter St. Teresa attempts to describe these two states on the basis of their effects. The first she calls in Spanish *contentos*, and the second *gustos*. They are hard words to translate. Fr. Kieran calls them respectively: consolations and spiritual delights. The older translation by Peers uses: sweetness and spiritual consolation. Literally I would call them joys and pleasures, except we may in English put joys above pleasures. In any case, the first is the result of our meditations and natural efforts at prayer from which we derive a certain satisfaction or an emotional relief like tears. Her best distinction is that the first type begins with us and ends in God, but the second begins with God and is felt by our human nature.

We are not talking about something relegated to the Fourth Mansion when we talk about the first of these—the *contentos*, because, as St. Teresa says they are many times experienced in the former mansions. We may all experience these sudden joys as a result of our efforts. The Fourth Mansion begins as a result of God's intervention. Usually a person remains a long time in the Third Mansion, before God brings him into the Fourth, if

48

ever. St. Teresa makes the remark that supernatural favors are not necessary for salvation. But if God wishes to bestow his favors, it is usually on those who have made some effort in prayer.

Temptations in this mansion are fewer, and less harmful, but St. Teresa thinks that the soul would be better off with a few than none at all, for the reason that it would be less likely to be deceived by these spiritual favors. Her analogy for temptations is those venomous creatures that she talked about before. In the rest of this first chapter, St. Teresa is very autobiographical. She explains how once she began weeping over the passion of Our Lord, she couldn't stop until it gave her a headache. But she wasn't sure whether it was emotional distress or a grace of God. She still counsels to love much rather than to think much, but in case we might think loving is an emotional experience, she clarifies what she means. "it is not in greater delight, but in greater determination of desiring to please God in everything" (Mansions IV,1,7). She adds to this, the avoidance of sin, the advancement of the honor and glory of Jesus, and the growth of the Catholic Church. This last is notable, coming from a woman of a totally Catholic culture, and who knew no other church. But we must remember that it had been only a short time before that the Church was firmly established in Spain, and even shorter that Luther inaugurated his revolt, to say nothing of the evangelization of the Americas. The Church for her was not a body politic, but Jesus alive in the world. One does not pray and have no concern for the Church, and that means the Catholic Church. Today one hears quite often, perhaps in an attempt to be ecumenical, the term Catholic Christian. Spain had 800 years of ecumenism, with Moors and Jews, yet in the Spanish language *Cristiano* and *Catolico* are interchangeable terms, Catholic is never an adjective.

St. Teresa spends the rest of this chapter talking about one of the most troublesome things we have to deal with in prayer. It was equally as troublesome for her, a cloistered nun with no television or radio! St. Teresa treats this same problem in chapter 17 of her *Life*, which, as she told us was written some 14 or 15 years previously. Actually she seems to have a better grasp of her subject in that work, even though she professes ignorance of the difference between her thoughts and her faculty called the intellect, in this Fourth Mansion; that is, until she

consulted a learned man, which she says was some four years
ago. It has been suggested this man was St. John of the Cross,
since he was her confessor at the time. Perhaps St. Teresa's
confusion comes from her idea, like ours, that the representa-
tions of the imagination and the memory should not be part of
our thinking process, but they are. And we are still more than
our thoughts. It was Descarte, whose basic premise was: "I
think therefore I am." We are spiritual beings, as well as bodies,
and we have spiritual powers called intellect and will, whether
they are in operation or not. If this were not so, then what are
we when we are asleep? What St. Teresa is finally saying is that
we can be united in prayer with God, even while our myriads of
silly thoughts and imaginations are churning about us. It was in
chapter 17 of her *Life* that she used the memorable figure of
moths flying around a candlelight as a comparison of these distractions. She also repeats and compares the process of thinking
to a mill which keeps on grinding—both in chapter 15 of her *Life*
and in this chapter.

There is also another distraction, which St. Teresa mentions, and these are the ringing and buzzing in her ears. She
doesn't seem to realize that these are completely physical and
perhaps a sign that she was going deaf. I do find it interesting
that she thought "the superior part of the soul was in the superior part of the head." We often think the people of her day
had no knowledge of the brain. Her mistake was to try and locate the soul where the thinking was going on. Our souls are
commensorate with our bodies, regardless of the division of our
activities. She should have drawn this conclusion, since she
admits that no afflictions bother her when her prayer is accompanied with suspension. This is the first indication that these
gustos from the Lord also take her out of her body, so to speak.

In the second chapter St. Teresa comes back to her topic,
excusing herself for any repetition, but she refuses to read over
what she has written to avoid it. This is not the ordinary
picture we have of great writers—all the more reason we have of
considering her writings as somewhat inspired. It is in this chapter that St. Teresa uses the metaphors of the aqueduct and the
spring. These two different types of prayer are often designated
as acquired and infused. To get water by means of an aqueduct
naturally requires a lot of labor, the spring nothing. This is the
difference between sweetness in prayer and the prayer that God

gives, which results in total absorption, like the times when seers are thrown to their knees, and talk to the Blessed Virgin.

Aqueducts are found all over Spain, and it was the Moors who first introduced irrigation to the West, so it comes as no surprise that St. Teresa should use this symbol. But this is not the only symbol she uses when describing the prayer of the Spring. Here she tells us that this prayer seems to permeate her whole being like incense in a room, and the source is from deep within—*el mas profundo centro del alma*, a concept found also in St. John of the Cross, and the German Mystics before him. Those who say they would rather go to the top of a mountain instead of a church to find God, have overlooked our Christian revelation, which says that we are temples of the Holy Spirit. One doesn't go anywhere except within in prayer.

The great difference between the consolations received from one's own labor and that of God is in the effect it has on the body. The first may cause, along with the delight, sobbing, nosebleeds, deafness, cramps in the chest or stomach, physical pain, and even (as we mentioned before in our study of St. John of the Cross) sexual arousal, since the body is trying to partake of what is essentially spiritual. Whereas, the gift of God takes over the body, and suspends its functions. This results in a deep recollection, and peace with very little thought of self.

Now if we cannot gain this second water, this gift of God, is it right to desire it or seek after it? St. Teresa gives five reasons for not seeking after the extraordinary in prayer. I will mention only the first because it is the most important, and that is to love God without self interest. Regardless of God's favors, humility and detachment are always to be practiced, probably because they are the exact opposite of what prompted the sin of Adam, and what caused the angels to fall.

In chapter three of this mansion, St. Teresa goes back to the original analogy of the Castle; she reminds us that our senses and faculties are the people of the castle. They have wandered about and gone outside the castle, but have not strayed too far. The King, who is now a Shepherd, calls them back very gently; they are usually those who have begun to despise the things of the world. It is here that St. Teresa mentions those in the married state, and makes a distinction between religious, who must give up the world in deed, but asks the married ones to surrender in desire. In other words it is an invitation to be attentive to interior matters. It is a gentle call to be in his presence. This is all leading up to what she calls the prayer of recollection, which does not require on our part discursive reasoning or meditations using the imagination. She writes this defensively, because there was a dispute about doing nothing at prayer and the warning of the Church against certain doctrines of the Quietists. What St. Teresa is talking about is the business of (in today's jargon) "letting go" when the Lord seems to be calling us to this stage of mindlessness. Today we hear much about listening in prayer from those who don't know what they are talking about. One listens only when God calls. That is why she warns us against the purposeful emptying of our thoughts. This is the danger that the Holy Office warned religious about in a recent letter concerning the use of Eastern techniques of prayer. I have mentioned this before, but these techniques have become so widespread in today's catechetics, and religious life. Things like Yoga, Transcendental Meditation, and all their accompanying positions, are natural practices that induce natural states, unless the Lord intervenes. St. Teresa uses as her authority St. Peter of Alcantara, and books like *The Ascent of Mount Sion*, written by Bernadino de Laredo. These were much-read authors of her day and they were being scrutinized by the Inquisition. Would that the authorities scrutinize more quickly today's authors on Prayer!

St. Teresa gives four reasons for her position: First, we are fools to try and induce this state, so we must use our faculties until the Lord makes it impossible. Second, since it is brought about by gentleness and peacefulness, anything forced (she mentions holding one's breath) is not going to work. Third, the psychological outcome of trying to suppress something usually causes the opposite: if we try not to use the mind, it will most likely go into high gear. And fourthly, it is the honor and glory of God we are seeking, and not some delightful state for ourselves.

In all this, St. Teresa is talking about the prayer of Recollection, which she says is really the beginning of the prayer of *gustos* (spiritual delight or pleasure). She also calls this the prayer of Quiet; it is a less intense contemplation, as compared to those periods of total absorption, and it corresponds to St. John of the Cross' chapters on the initial stages of contemplation, outlined in the *Ascent of Mount Carmel*, book II, chapter

13 and the following.

St. Teresa then gives the effects or the signs of this type of prayer. They are not analogical as those of St. John of the Cross. He gives only three signs: 1) lack of satisfaction with meditation; 2) disinclination to use the imagination, and; 3) preference for remaining alone with God. I count about six signs of St. Teresa. They are: 1) the feeling of greater freedom, and less servile fear toward God. 2) A greater desire to do penance, and less concern for bodily health. 3) A livelier faith and the desire to do something for God. 4) A greater knowledge of God's grandeur, accompanied by a corresponding humility. 5) A greater detachment from the world and its joys. 6) An improvement of all the virtues.

This chapter ends with two strong warnings. The first of these is backsliding, especially by putting oneself in the occasion of sin and withdrawing from prayer. This no doubt comes from St. Teresa's own experience which she tells us about in her *Life* in chapter 7. She makes the observation that the devil is especially busy with these souls, because he sees they are God's friends. If they go astray, they stray farther than others. We see this very thing happening today among priests and religious, and especially in convents into feminism.

The other warning, she directs against those who have reached this stage of prayer, especially women, because they are of a weaker constitution, so she says. This is a type of rapture or swoon caused not by God, but by physical weakness or too much penance. Her remedy is to feed them, take them off prayer and put them to work. She does not accuse them of deception but perhaps of a lack of prudence.

This is a very crucial mansion because it is here that the natural and the supernatural come together. Many enter, but even more retreat.

Fifth Mansions: Prayer of Union
The Silkworm and the Butterfly
(Chapters 1-2)

In this Fifth Mansion, we are now entering upon a state that is reserved for the truly serious and devout person of prayer. St. Teresa seems to be contradictory about how rare this is. Even her passage in Spanish is hard to decipher. She says *most* (meaning those who practice prayer) get inside the mansion, but *few* will attain all the benefits. So we must conclude that there are many degrees within this mansion. At the same time, we should consider ourselves greatly favored by God to have reached the door of the mansion.

What we are discussing in this mansion is what is called the Prayer of Union, which goes beyond the Prayer of Quiet of the Fourth Mansion. Most of the first two chapters deals with St. Teresa's attempt to explain just what it is, because she is trying to explain something that happens which is beyond our two faculties of understanding and will, and beyond our emotional life—something completely spiritual. Whatever is spiritual is beyond figure and forms, there she is left to analogy.

I was given some articles from today's tabloids in which the authors claimed to have taken pictures of the human soul departing from the body, and another, that of some baby's guardian angel! Without a special manifestation on the part of God, spiritual substances do not lend themselves to physical portrayal.

In the prayer of union, we have definitely entered into contemplation. It is here that St. Teresa reminds her sisters that, as Carmelites, they are called to a life of prayer and contemplation. There is no doubt that St. Teresa was conscious of the Carmelite Order, and of its purpose within the Church. There are those who claim that she did not have a full grasp of what she was about and that she was in favor of more missionary and apostolic activity. It is hard to reconcile that opinion with her references to the Carmelites of Old, which are always to the hermits and never to the mendicant situation they later adapted. She says: "for this was our origin, from this race did we come, from those holy Fathers of ours of Mount Carmel who in such great solitude, and with such contempt for the world, sought this precious pearl of which we are speaking" (prayer and contemplation) (Mansions V, 1, 2).

She goes on to tell us that we don't reach contemplation if we fail to dispose ourselves especially in the practice of virtue. Unlike false mysticism, and those who propose methods of obtaining a contemplative state, St. Teresa's contemplation comes from holiness of life; she tells us at this point all techniques are not only superfluous, they are useless because all the faculties have been suspended—asleep as it were, but not in the dreamy state of the Prayer of Quiet. If you have read about the experiments done on the seers of Medjugorje, you will recognize that they are actually in a state of contemplation similar to what St. Teresa describes here. They do not move nor respond to bodily disturbance. God has given them a glimpse of the other world, where the body cannot follow nor grasp; it is left with only a residual delight from the experience of the soul.

In the Fifth Mansion no poisonous creatures can enter, that is there are no temptations or disturbances, simply because the extent of the devil's field is the body and its functions, which include the imagination. Since all these functions are suspended, there is peace. For the person who has experienced this prayer of union, there is no need to explain further, but since St. Teresa is writing for all of us, she tells us that the difference between Union and the Prayer of Quiet is like the difference between feeling something in the marrow of the bones and something on the surface of the skin. She put great confidence in learned men who attempt to explain these mystical states—as long as they do not lead a dissipated life. In other words, she puts her trust in those who are open to the ways of God and have attempted to follow this way of grace. St. Teresa is wary of those who do not practice what they preach, because she is not sure they are being guided by the Holy Spirit. Following this line of thinking, can we really trust people like Martin Luther or Henry VIII, whose moral lives were hardly exemplary?

Next, St. Teresa discusses how a soul who has experienced this union can have such great certitude of its truth, especially when she admits that it does not understand it. She goes on to explain how God can be present in the soul and impart this certitude. It is here also that she gives us an example of misguided direction by an unlearned priest. We must recall that these were the days before the decrees of the Council of Trent regarding the organization of seminaries were put into effect. So many priests had only a minimum of theology. Although he had three years of philosophy, even St. John of the Cross had only one year of theology before ordination. We know he made up for that, but many did not. I would say there is somewhat of a parallel today, where in our seminaries there is a minimum of philosophy, and theology comes across as a bunch of opinions. Our priests are more comfortable with sociological and psychological problems than with mystical prayer.

St. Teresa mentions this same incident in her *Life.* Here she adds the name of the Order of the priest who set her straight about the presence of God in the soul. It was the Dominican Order, and Fr. Gracian, who corrected the manuscript revealed the name of the priest in the margin. It was Fr. Vicente Barron, one of her earlier confessors, who knew his Thomistic philosophy. We have gone over this point before, where we mentioned that God is present in the soul by his presence, power and essence, as well as by grace. In a sense this is the whole point of this treatise, that is, how God resides in the soul—in the very center, she says, and how we proceed to find him through prayer.

She had one warning for the skeptic, and there are altogether too many of those among us, especially the clergy or parish activists. In any case, she says that those who doubt that God can or will grant other and greater favors to us have effectively closed the door to them. She urges us to expect more of God, not less, but at the same time it would be for our benefit not to expect to understand these mystical favors. St. Teresa was under obedience to attempt an explanation of all that she was favored with. God no doubt gave her many favors so that she would do this. Today we have a whole school of people who advocate journaling. In view of what St. Teresa says, I have my reservations about this, and its usefulness to one's prayer life. It can result in too much self-absorption and the trivialization of God's deeper favors.

In the second chapter of this Fifth Mansion, St. Teresa explains the various degrees of union as being of intensity. To explain these she brings up her now-famous simile of the silkworm—how from small eggs in the sunshine the worm hatches out, eats and buries itself in a cocoon, dies and is transformed into a butterfly. This is, of course, the life, death and resurrection sequence applied to that of prayer. It is a famous analogy and many have waxed eloquent about it. However, like most analogies, it limps. The egg turned worm is the soul, which with some difficulty wraps itself in Christ or God, and it then dies in Christ to itself and is raised up into a new and exciting existence in the spiritual life. What makes this somewhat confusing is the initial analogy of the Castle, where God dwells in the center of the soul. Now she has the soul dwelling in the house of God; in other words the castle is the soul in one analogy, and the cocoon is God in the other. But in either case the point she makes is that the soul grows in Christ through its own efforts by taking away from itself all that is not God, that is, by being detached and doing penance, etc. When the soul is dead to itself, it is released as a white butterfly. In the cocoon the soul is immersed in God. This then is the Prayer of Union, and the butterfly is the soul after it has experienced this prayer. It comes forth renewed and different. It is a beautiful analogy, but not all that coherent if we measure it by plain reason, which I suppose, she would not let us do anyway.

The new state of this soul is one of zeal, that is zeal for the things of God; it wants to praise God, perform great penances, to suffer great trials for him, and lastly to be alone in solitude. All these things if you will recall are the same as those St. John of the Cross mentioned about a soul who has reached contemplation. Another thing which St. John mentioned is that it now finds life wearisome, and all creatures tiresome, even relatives and friends. Now I know that this will seem strange to us who have been instructed to love our relatives and friends; it will horrify the social-action crowd. And the tendency is to doubt the authenticity of such a state. But we can understand this only by realizing that once a person has had a touch of the divinity, all else is pale and meaningless. So the soul suffers the absence of God between his short states of this Prayer of Union, and they are at this period only short experiences, no more than one half hour. Although the soul does experience a deep peace, it is still troubled by not being able to do more, and by the offenses of others towards God. As St. Teresa remarks, a few years ago all the soul could think of was itself, and now it is concerned with universal salvation. So we see the view that the contemplative life is a selfish pursuit, does not bear the truth. The more one loves God, the more is he concerned with the plight of all humanity. It is here that the soul sees the redeeming value of suffering, and in its own ability to unite one's suffering with those of Christ. Let me quote this phrase from St. Teresa which counteracts the fundamentalist notion that Christ has suffered once and for all, so that our sufferings have no redeeming value. She says "and so as it has been he who has paid the higher cost, so he wants to join our little labors with the great ones His Majesty suffered so that all may be one thing" (Mansions V, 2, 5).

The last paragraph of this second chapter is a touching meditation on the sufferings of Christ over the offences committed against God. It is a paragraph that needs to be read by this generation which has forgotten that anything offends God. The other day I heard confessions for two hours, and nothing was confessed that I would consider a mortal sin. Most of it dealt with human relations. Either these were exceptionally good young people, or they haven't been taught what sin is. I would prefer to believe the former, but I want to shout from the housetops that sin has to do with a person and God, not between one person and another. The contemplative person does not become wary and judgmental but he does begin to see the gravity of offending God, simply because he begins to see the holiness of God, thus he suffers with Christ over the sins of mankind. This in itself is a grace, and all the guilt-ridden people would be far better off going to confession, than to see a psychiatrist. The person who is aware of the offences against God, sees first of all how he himself has also offended and keeps on offending a merciful and forgiving God.

Martin Luther who knew that he offended God came across a novel way to rid himself of guilt, and every Protestant suffers from it since. He has God covering over our offences by his death, so that a soul is not purified of sin, but cloaked from it. This is a far cry from the teaching of St. Teresa. It is only when we have learned the meaning of suffering, that we have learned the meaning of Christianity.

Fifth Mansions: Prayer of Union

Love is not Idle

(Chapters 3-4)

In this third chapter of the Fifth Mansion, St. Teresa comes back to her analogy of the silkworm. Actually she says "little dove," but she uses little dove and little butterfly interchangeably with a certain feminine affection. Again it is not clear in St. Teresa's rambling how this analogy applies. But she seems to say that one who has set herself on this road, must be careful not to turn back. Once she has had a taste of this union, though, and become lax, there are still certain elements in her life that can benefit others, even when they have not benefitted herself. Just as the silkworm eventually produces other silkworms, but in the process dies, the same can happen to us. She seems to use the death of the silkworm both in a bad sense and in a good sense. If we stray we die to our spiritual life, but in the spiritual life we die to ourselves.

She gives an example of a person who grew lax and gave up her prayer-life. Whenever St. Teresa says, "I knew a person" she is usually referring to herself. She says, "being very lost, she liked to benefit others with the mercy God had granted her and to show the road to prayer to those who did not understand it and she did sufficient good, indeed" (Mansions V, 3, 2). In this passage St. Teresa is probably referring to the role she played in setting her own father on the road to prayer, even after she had fallen from the way of prayer herself. This she recounts in her autobiography in chapter seven, where she also mentions others as well. "It was not only he, but some other persons that I influenced to practice prayer" (Life VII, 13). She would give them books and show them how to make meditation, which she credits to her initial prayer-life, even though she had now dropped it. This explains what she says here: "and even when they have already lost it, it happens to remain with that desire to benefit others" (Mansions V, 3, 1).

Now she goes on to say that it is possible to enter this mansion even without the supernatural favors that often accompany it. So she distinguishes between two types of union—the first

59

being the total resignation of the will to God, and the second is the "delightful union." The first is what we can do (with the ordinary help of God) to want what God wants in our life. In the doctrine of St. John this is the active night, which requires the practice of virtue and the negation of self. The second is the infused prayer of union or what God does to the soul that has prepared itself. She says, "one is not able to arrive at the said union if the union of our will in being resigned to that of God is not very certain" (Mansions V, 3, 3).

In either case there are still sufferings and consolations during this stage, but they do not reach the depth of the higher mansions, and they come and go quickly. This union of wills is what St. Teresa says she has desired all her life, and she admits there are few who reach it. The reason for this does not lie in the commission of great sins, but rather in our laxity when it comes to practicing charity towards others, which denotes self-esteem. She clarifies this by relieving us of the notion that we should be apathetic in the face of emotional trials, such as pain or grief. In other words she does not want to rob us of our humanity, after all Jesus cried at the death of Lazarus. The most certain sign that we are conforming ourselves to the will of God is our love of neighbor. We can't always know how much we love God, but there is little doubt about how much we love our neighbor, and this in turn shows us how much we love God. Furthermore, she makes it clear that she is not talking about grand schemes in the service of one's neighbor—We don't all have that kind of resources; she is talking about our reaction to the person next to us. The other Mother Teresa of our day started out washing the bodies of those she found in the streets of Calcutta. From this small beginning she is now reaching out to the world.

Though she talks of devotion and experience, St. Teresa makes it very clear where one's duty lies. The needs of others come first. "Works is what the Lord wants" (Mansions V, 3, 11). One does not delight in her spiritual delights and ignore a sick sister, in the interest of the Prayer of Union. This statement is in direct contrast to her dissident contemporary, Martin Luther, whose battle cry was "faith without works."

We can take the two extremes and find ourselves equally mistaken. St. Teresa is not advocating wandering around looking for good works to avoid prayer. It is the same teaching of

Our Lord who did not find it in the interest of serving God to leave the ox or the ass in the pit during the sabbath. She treats of this subject in her book of the *Foundations* (chap. 5, 17), where she says, "It is necessary to act with prudence in not neglecting the matter of works even if it be obedience and charity which many times do not respond interiorly to your God." She devotes a chapter to the love her sisters must have for one another in her convent in her book *The Way of Perfection*, and it was to this that she was referring when she says, "I have said much in other places about this (Mansions V, 3, 12). In this paragraph at the end of chapter 3 of the *Interior Castle*, she sums it up in these words, "and force your will to do in everything the will of your sisters, even though you lose your rights and forget your well being for hers" (Mansions V, 3, 12). How far we are from this ideal; how far we are from the Prayer of Union.

In this last chapter of the Fifth Mansion, St. Teresa again refers to the little dove, meaning the little butterfly of her silkworm analogy. It has been almost five months since she has written anything on it, as she says. She had moved from Toledo to Avila. It is amazing how she was able to continue her train of thought, or maybe this is why she starts another comparison, even though she promises to come back to the analogy of the butterfly. This new comparison is that of the ritual of betrothal as practiced in the 16th-century Spain. She continues this into the next mansion. In the arrangement for marriage there were six stages: 1) meetings between the man and woman; 2) the exchange of gifts; 3) time to fall in love; 4) the joining of hands; 5) betrothal; 6) marriage. The girl was usually chaperoned throughout this process. In the case of the titled the marriage was often arranged, thus the need for a time to fall in love.

In the third paragraph of this chapter, St. Teresa calls her comparison a course one, and she evidently feels the need to make it clear that she is talking about spiritual realities, and not the pleasures of the married life. It was in vogue at the time to use the sumbol of marriage and the romance connected with it, especially as found in the biblical *Song of Songs;* and the Holy Office was especially cautious about this symbolism in view of the excesses of the Quietist heresy, which said there was nothing wrong in indulging the senses, after a person had reached the contemplative state.

While she makes it clear that this Prayer of Union has not reached the stage of betrothal, for that is the subject matter of the Sixth Mansion, she does mention that the Prayer of Union is like these meetings between lovers so that they will get to know each other better; they are short, very effective, and so revealing that she skips the exchange of gifts. And the divine love of the spouse-to-be makes the future bride more worthy of the joining of hands. She doesn't belabor these stages, but only points to them for an audience who was very familiar with them. Spanish-speaking Carmelites have many times indicated that their Anglo-Saxon cousins do not completely grasp the full expression of St. Teresa's writings. There is something to be said for this contention, but to get bogged down in cultural niceties, on the other hand, and ignore the central message is not beneficial either.

The rest of this chapter is devoted more or less to an admonition to those people who have come to this union, that they avoid the occasions of sin. Again this is in direct contrast to the Quietists, who think they are beyond sin at this stage. According to St. Teresa, the soul is still not strong enough, and through negligence it can fall. The devil fights with all his might to keep the soul from the stage of betrothal; it is out of his reach. On this point St. Teresa seems to be contradicting herself, because in chapter one of this mansion, she declared that the devil could not enter or do any harm here, and that the poisonous creatures cannot enter. The only explanation I can think of is that this stage of union is not continuous. During the periods of union, the devil cannot interfere, but at other times he can. In any case she points to the stage of betrothal as the state which effectively excludes the devil.

Getting ahead of herself, she mentions how the martyrs and founders of Religious Orders, whom she presumes to have reached the stage of betrothal, have brought many souls to heaven. She mentions St. Dominic and St. Francis and Fr. Ignatius; the last of these founded his Jesuits only about 30 years before she founded the first convent of the reform. As an interesting footnote, St. Teresa's first reviser of her texts, Fray Luis de Leon purposely omitted any mention of Ignatius in this passage. Ordinarily he restored the text of St. Teresa from the corrections of her Provincial. It seems Fray Luis, an Augustinian, was involved in a lawsuit between the University of Salamanca, where he taught, and the Jesuits!

St. Teresa acknowledges that she had known people of a high degree of spirituality who have lost the whole thing because they have set their affections on something less than God. Here she poses two questions: How can a soul who has followed the will of God be deceived, and how does the devil gain access to such a soul? To the first she answers that souls who through the guise of doing good can get into practices that they see as not wrong, and through their own deception fall out of grace little by little. This is so true of formerly religious people of today, especially those who have accepted unconditional change as a way of life. They are too ready to throw out what has been traditionally accepted—especially those things of a moral nature. These are the ones who reject the distinction between mortal and venial sin; they persuade themselves that the laws of the Church are things from the past.

To the second question, she tells us that the Lord may wish to try a soul whom he has set up as an example to others, and permits the devil to tempt him. Better that he fall alone than drag others with him later on. She reminds us that Judas was in close contact with the Lord himself, yet he fell.

She is convinced that a soul who is constantly watchful, who never completely trusts himself, and prays for perseverance will be given many interior warnings if it is about to go wrong. No one is handed over to the devil; we know in cases of possession persons are gradually drawn into his net. That is why we must not dabble in the unknown and the forbidden. I read of a case where a young lady was at first shocked when her old teddy-bear began to speak with her; she threw it out only to find it back in her apartment; it continued to speak with her until she began to speak back and eventually carried on conversations. Innocent enough we may think, until it urged her to do harm to herself. After seeking help, she was finally exorcised. In the beginning she admitted she played with the Ouiji board. A dramatic case to prove the insinuations of the devil!

A final sign to those who have reached this stage of prayer that something is wrong is the soul's lack of advancement and growth. "Love is not idle," she says. Beware the "its time I was good to myself" syndrome. Preoccupation with one's own needs to the detriment of the needs of others, whether in the physical or the spiritual, would be a bad sign in any stage. As a last challenge she reminds us that our own trivial pursuits and sufferings are nothing compared to our reward through the mercy of God.

Her last paragraph is a long prayer that she may be able to benefit others through these writings that she was commanded to do.

To sum up what this Fifth Mansion is all about: the soul has reached contemplative prayer, or as St. Teresa explains it, the Prayer of Union, where God begins to reveal himself to the soul in a deeper way; the intellect and the will are made captive for short periods of time. God is preparing the soul for what she calls the Betrothal. At this stage (which is crucial) the soul undergoes trials of the spirit, temptations to return by occasions of sin, which are more subtle than before, and for some, illness and scruples. It is at this time that it finds itself misunderstood and even harassed by good people.

St. Teresa was at this door early in life and she fell away for 18 years, not by committing big sins, but by ignoring her better judgment and ceasing to engage in mental prayer. She insists so strongly on the avoidance of occasions of sin, because she so long dabbled with them in her idle conversations with the young men of Avila, and in her gossip within her community. The Lord waited patiently for her to return. With some effort, we can all reach this mansion, but what follows will be up to God.

Sixth Mansions: Spiritual Betrothal
Transverberation
(Chapters 1-3)

We come now to the largest treatment of prayer in the *Interior Castle* of St. Teresa. It deals with a stage of prayer that few of us reach, and we may wonder why she wrote eleven chapters describing something that would benefit so few. As you know, it deals with what the mystics call spiritual betrothal. We will notice that the lines marking out the Fifth and Sixth Mansions are not so clearly divided. The spiritual betrothal seems to occur within this Sixth Mansion, and not as the dividing line itself. The spiritual betrothal results as a consequence of the meeting and falling in love already mentioned. The Lord wishes to confirm this love by sending even greater trials and misfortunes, as he did to Job, before taking her as his spouse. So in this first section St. Teresa treats of these difficulties, and later on of the great benefits and the types of experience it may encounter.

One of the first trials she mentions is no doubt autobiographical. Here she talks of the gossip about persons who begin to have mystical experiences, and warns even her confessors to beware of her. Our tendency is always to look for self-delusion in a person that claims to have visions or some other phenomenon out of the ordinary. As St. Teresa says, most people abhor such things. It goes without saying that this person can expect persecution even from the good. Praise for such a person is equally troublesome, until that soul begins to ignore what other people say altogether. I would say this is perhaps more difficult for a woman whose nature is to want to appear attractive, than to a man, but not in every case; vanity has no gender!

In one way praise for a person's supposed holiness is a greater trial than outright persecution, so that a soul prefers and even looks for persecution in the light of the Lord's sufferings. That is why St. Thérèse was able to love Mother Gonzague, who hounded her into sanctity.

Going on her own experience, St. Teresa tells us that the soul which has reached this stage also experiences physical pains as well as spiritual ones. We know that St. Teresa came down with some strange illnesses, and that for many years would wake up with nausea and vomiting. Of course some sceptics would attribute all this to psychiatric problems. But we must recognize that the body simply cannot accommodate itself to the mystical graces that God gives to the soul. The Medjugorje seer, Vicka, suffered a mysterious illness for some time, which she said was from God. So too, do Stigmatics suffer vicariously for the sins of the world. These Christians who insist that a good God would never allow us to suffer do not understand what it means to be a friend of a Crucified Jesus. There are some here today who are being asked to bear a giant's share in suffering for the sins of the world, and this is the best way to look at it. You will not go unrewarded.

But St. Teresa is more concerned over the mental trials she had to undergo because of deficient counsellors and confessors, who counselled her in ignorant ways. One thought she was being deluded by the devil, and he told her to give her vision "the fig," which I imagine was something like "giving it the finger!" She did it in obedience with tears in her eyes. And one of her biggest trials was her inability to explain what she was experiencing, and in her confusion she would even warn her confessors to beware of being deceived by herself. That must really have helped them! The Seers at Garabandal also at one time in a fit of confusion and scrupulosity denied having had their visions—a denial Our Lady had already predicted.

It is at this time that the soul reaches an all-time low in its estimation of itself and its love for God. We might legitimately ask why this torment now? St. Teresa gives us the answer: "This great God wants us to know our need and that he is King, and this matters a lot for what lies ahead" (Mansions VI, 1, 12). She tells us that mental prayer is next to impossible, and both, being with people and seeking solitude are equally a torment. She elaborates on this in her autobiography, where she says that she wanted to snap at everybody, and they could all see she was suffering, and gloomy. What a way to end all this previous effort; it's as if a soul had regressed to the point of beginning, except that it is firmly established in virtue. What does it do now? She says: "the best remedy is to attend to works of charity and external things and to hope in the mercy of God who never fails those who hope in him" (Mansions VI, 1, 13).

She mentions at least three times that all this is in preparation for entering the Seventh and highest Mansion, which means also that she regards this Sixth Mansion as transitional. This would make sense, since betrothal leads to marriage.

In this second chapter, St. Teresa tries to explain an experience which, either during or after this aforementioned torment, comes upon it suddenly and without any effort on the soul's part. I would say it is like the feeling of a young man, who has fallen in love; he is overwhelmed with delight, but at the same time his heart aches causing a pain that he wishes would never go away. We must translate this to the spiritual order, where things are even more acute. She can attribute this experience to no faculty that she possesses; it seems to come from the depths of her being, or from God himself. Unlike other mystical experiences, she does not doubt its authenticity. On the lower plane, what young lover would ever question his falling in love? And I would say true love is pure and holy, and never are lovers more inclined to share their love with God! Young people with conquest or experiences on their mind, which lead to improper intimacies are full of desire, and not love. This sex-saturated society has lost something very essential. Remember we are still in the stage of betrothal. Although we are speaking of higher things, we must always recognize that there are vestiges of the higher in the lower, because we are made in God's image.

What St. Teresa is explaining in this chapter is what we call her Transverberation, where her heart was pierced with a fiery dart from heaven. Both this and the divine impulses from God are better explained in her autobiography in chapter 29. Here she describes it in these words:

> "I saw an angel near me toward the left side in bodily form . . . he was not tall but short, very beautiful . . .he must be those who are called cherubim . . . I saw in his hands a long golden arrow and at the tip of the iron head, it seemed to have a small fire. This, it seemed, he plunged into my heart several times so that it reached my entrails. On withdrawing it, it seemed he carried them with it, and he left me totally afire in a great love for God" (Life XXIX, 13).

Padre Pio and numerous other saints also went through a similar mystical experience, which seems to be a stage of prayer that precedes the Seventh Mansion, or in some cases, as in that of Padre Pio, the stigmata, where the subject is imprinted with the wounds of Christ. This also is described as a definite wound, which causes pain. St. Teresa says that "It feels it is wounded exquisitely . . . it knows it is a precious thing and never wants to be healed of that wound . . . it is full of pain although delightful and sweet" (Mansions VI, 2, 2). Padre Pio wrote this: "From that day onward, I have been mortally wounded. I feel in the depths of my soul a wound that is always open and which causes me continual agony" (Letter to Padre Benedetto, August 21, 1918—quoted by Michael Freze, *"They Bore the Wounds of Christ,"* Huntington: OS Visitor, 1989, p. 168).

The souls chosen to receive these special graces of God are either victim souls that are chosen to suffer for those many who need God's grace, or they are chosen to bear the image of the Crucified for the example of us all. Many of us would like to partake of the delights of the high forms of prayer, but not too many realize the price one must pay. It is in the Gospel for all of us to see "Unless you take up your cross and follow me, you cannot be my disciple." This is a far cry from today's emphasis on a happy fraternity of playful Christians! The sacrifice of Christ on the cross is an essential message of the Gospel, and to empty this symbol of the Crucified one, as some have done in our Chruches, and to replace it with the Resurrected Christ in the interest of being always positive is to miss the meaning of suffering, which will never go away as long as we are alive. I might add, it is this unreality that Protestantism has brought to Christianity, so that people abhor and try to avoid suffering as of no value or purpose.

Another point that St. Teresa makes in this chapter is the reason why a soul feels secure in this experience as not coming from the devil. She gives three reasons. The first is the most important, and it deals with the experience itself—the inability of the devil to bring together both pain and pleasure at once. His pleasure is usually of the emotional kind and his pain causes not delight, but confusion. Secondly, the origin of this experience is obviously from deep within, and out of his range. And thirdly, the result of the experience leads one to want to suffer for God, and withdraw from earthly things.

The last paragraph of this chapter contains a more delightful experience in this stage of prayer, almost as if St. Teresa doesn't want to leave us with the idea that all was now suffering without respite. Here she describes a feeling which comes over all the senses to confirm the fact that the presence of her Spouse is basically one of delight. She compares it to one of a delightful fragrance permeating her senses from deep within. It is only by way of analogy she speaks, because in her book called the *Relaciones*, she says, "When I see something beautiful, plentiful like water, fields, flowers, fragrances, music, etc., it seems I wouldn't want to see nor hear them, so much is the difference between it and what I am accustomed to see and thus the desire for them is taken away" (Relations 1, 11). It is not her intention to disdain the beautiful; but when one is in possession of the all-Beautiful, things pale before It.

In chapter three, St. Teresa treats entirely of the different kinds of locutions. Locutions are a communication from God or a spiritual being to a soul either by means of the sense of hearing in words, or through the imagination, or directly to the intellect in concepts. St. John of the Cross outlined for us three kinds of locutions: successive, formal and substantial. Successive is the result of one's own meditations and deep thoughts, and we might categorize them as an enlightenment of the Holy Spirit, which many times they are, but they can be nothing more than our own intellectual musings or from the devil; these are from within. Formal locutions come from an outside source; these may take the form of audible words, or interior words, containing a message either for oneself or for others. Substantial locutions also come from without; they also can be words, or an impressed understanding of something dealing with the Faith, but they produce what they say. For instance, if you were to hear the words, "Be joyful!" you would immediately be joyful.

St. Teresa deals with these types of locutions from her own experience, and less in the academic treatment of St. John. She tells us: "Some seem to come from outside, others from the very interior of the soul, others from the superior part of it, others so exterior that they are heard with the ears, because it seems to be a formed sound" (Mansions VI, 3, 1). Before discussing these different types of locutions, she gives a general warning to those who have this sort of thing, to be wary of them, regardless of their origin, whether from God or the devil. This is the same advice as that of St. John of the Cross.

St. Teresa was concerned with this topic probably because she lived in a time when there was a greater manifestation of phenomena of this type, as there is in our own age, when we hear of visionaries with messages from so many prayer groups. How we can distinguish the true from the false? First of all by the personality of the subject himself or herself. She was aware of overly pious, and emotionally unstable persons who heard voices, especially of the audible kind, and thought most of these had an overly active imagination, and she counselled superiors to keep them occupied in more active pursuits for their own sakes, lest the devil take over their lives.

A true locution must not teach anything against Holy Scripture. She mentions three signs that would indicate that it is authentic: 1) it must have power and authority; 2) it leaves the soul with great peace; 3) the words are engraven upon the memory. This then conforms to St. John's category of "substantial locution" and produces what it says. When it comes to messages which are given either to the soul or to others, she insists that they are to be submitted to the Keys, that is, to a confessor, and if the Lord wishes the message to be spread, he will see to it that the confessor comes to believe in it. This brings out a very important point. When Our Lord gave the Keys to Peter, he was in effect submitting even his ways to those of the Church in Faith and Morals. Even Our Lady obeyed the bishop in Garabandal, when he forbade the seers to have their visions in the parish church. Our Lady never appeared there again. St. Teresa submitted all her experiences to her confessor, and many times was as equally confused by him as by the experience itself. It is for this reason that she considers this one of the biggest trials in this stage of prayer; this is mentioned in the first chapter.

Locutions that come from the imagination, do not have the aforementioned signs, and as St. Teresa says, in the former prayer of quiet, souls can be lulled into thinking that they hear voices, especially if they have been asking the Lord for certain things or wanting to tell the world where it is wrong. We have all heard of an impending chastisement of mankind from the Fatima apparitions. There could be many souls who would want to elaborate on that. A locution purely from the imagination, will tell that soul what it wants to hear.

Most of St. Teresa's locutions and visions were of an intellectual nature, so she is more interested in explaining this and she gives five reasons why there is such certitude of their authenticity. Something of an intellectual nature by-passes the ordinary mode of thinking, which consists of the perceptions of an individual object through one of the five senses; this is impressed on the imagination, which forms a picture or a word, and from that the mind relates it to an abstract concept, which in turn relates it back to the individual thing perceived, so that a person *knows* with certitude what it sees. Modern philosophers have told us that we do not know things, but that we can only know what is in our minds. This erroneous teaching leads us to pure subjectivism, which is rampant in the world today. And in this way of thinking all knowledge becomes opinion, and we are then completely divorced from the outside world; we are minds wandering around in something we cannot be a part of.

Now it is possible for the Lord to give us direct knowledge of some truth, without going through this ordinary process of knowing. This is the type of locution St. Teresa is talking about. To put it in today's jargon, the soul has a direct printout, without having pushed the button. The message is received: 1) clearly, without variation or vagueness. This has been the experience of many seers with a message to the world. The little ignorant seers of La Salette repeated their same story over and over again without variation. 2) It is about things previously unknown and unexpected. 3) One hears the message, and does not compose it. 4) The message is impressed and immediate. 5) There is almost total comprehension put in words. She admits that the devil can counterfeit some locutions, but he cannot counterfeit the effects of a true locution.

Together with those we have already mentioned, humility and the new awareness of sin are absolutely necessary. Fear of the Lord and gratitude are others, together with confidence in the mercy of God.

The last objection, which St. Teresa says comes from people who don't have locutions is that the soul should distract itself from such things. To this she replies that it is impossible when the Lord intervenes, because he takes over one's faculties. In many cases the seers of Our Lady have been irresistably drawn to certain spots with a swiftness that cannot be duplicated by walking or running.

Now what do we do about all these people today who claim to be having locutions? How can we tell whether they are authentic? For the most part, we must recognize that St. Teresa is not talking about locutions that are meant for the public. But in those, she is explicit about how they are to be submitted to one's confessor. She makes no mention of a Bishop's authority over such matters, and today perhaps we are too conscious of the Bishop, and too unaware of the spiritual authority of an ordinary priest. Our Lady of Guadalupe sent Juan Diego to the Bishop; the matter involved the whole population. But Our Lady of Lourdes sent Bernadette to the parish priest. As long as an apparition or locution is pending approval, it can be taken seriously, but when it has been condemned by the Bishop (even if it is from the Lord) we are obligated to abide by the authorities. Such is the case with Necedah and Bayside.

These people who are receiving communications from variour prayer-groups, ought to be wary of deception. I have read some messages that sound like what we would like to hear— condemnation of evil people, and destruction of evil cities, and in some cases they are very specific. Ordinarily Our Lady is not specific in her messages: they are meant for all. Our Lady does not meddle in liturgical matters (sometimes I wish she would) but she may say things like "certain practices offend Our Lord"; nor does she leave us only with a negative message without giving us hope. These apocolyptic times demand caution against false prophets. If there is one thing that points to authenticity in these locutions, it is good language; heaven doesn't use slang or inclusive language, or technical terms or a complicated sentence structure. The Gospels are our model, and simplicity is the mark of holiness.

Sixth Mansions:
Spiritual Betrothal
Raptures, Ecstasies, Transports

(Chapters 4-6)

In chapter four of this Sixth Mansion St. Teresa begins her treatment of the extraordinary phenomena of these higher states of prayer. Most of this material is autobiographical, and we find it in a more detailed form in her previous book called her *Life* *(Vida* in Spanish). She is now writing under orders from her provincial, Fr. Gracian, who wanted a more ordered exposition of prayer for the benefit of others. Up to this point, she has described many of the trials and sufferings that go with the practice of prayer; she has also hinted at the rare delights one will encounter, but most of it can be explained by our psychological states, and human longings for love. She even warns those of a delicate constitution, not to be too quick to identify their feelings and swoons with the results of prayer. And some she advocates remaining in the called lower forms of prayer, that is, to continue in their meditations and activities for the benefit of their mental health. This does not mean these people are not called to sanctity; it means they are not called to the extraordinary.

As we said before, this mansion is about the spiritual betrothal. To conclude this betrothal, according to St. Teresa, God begins to give the soul ecstasies or raptures, where the spiritual part of man takes over, and leaves the senses behind. Since this experience goes beyond the senses, it can be explained only by analogy, and St. Teresa is hard-pressed to explain it. But she feels that she must try. After reading the chapter through, it is doubtful that we know any more about what it is, especially when she keeps on insisting that she can't describe it. She does tell us that it is a higher, more spiritual state than what is experienced in the prayer of quiet, where one becomes abstracted to a degree from his surroundings. We can all do that when we are intently busy about something. For instance an artist can lose track of time while he is engaged in his art work. This happens in meditations so that your prayer takes you away to the point of your meditations. But this is done by the mind itself. This is what St. Teresa was describing in the prayer of quiet. She emphatically declares that this is not what a rapture is. Nor is it any swooning-away with sensible feelings of love, or something that simply takes your breath away. These are by no means to be belittled; they are not what she is talking about.

For all of its lack of attention in today's theology, perhaps raptures are at the heart of most people's longing. We say that man was made for happiness. We know that this world cannot give us unlimited happiness. But there are some who try to find it here. There is a certain ecstasy in sex, but it is soon spent. Drugs take one into another wonderous, unreal world, where one is without care. But the after-effects can be a hell on earth. The same is true of alcohol. In seeking pleasure, one is attempting to escape this world and its afflictions. So it is rapture we are looking for, but in the wrong places. Just think if the populace could be convinced that it is possible (but only with the help of God) to attain a true rapture, how many contemplatives we would have. But who of us wants to undergo the necessary afflictions to obtain them?

Rapture comes quickly and without any help on our part; it is as if the soul were removed from the body; the person is dead to his senses. St. Teresa speaks of two different kinds of rapture. In this chapter, she mentions the first of these, which she gives no name to. (The other is called "flight of the spirit," which she treats of in the next chapter.) This rapture is caused by a word or memory of something about God; it leaves the soul with some perception of what is going on about it at first. This passes into a state of complete abstraction, where it is awakened to a greater understanding of the Divine. While in this state of suspension, God gives it either an imaginative vision about heavenly things or an intellectual vision of himself. The imaginative vision, since it was impressed upon the imagination, she could describe to a certain degree. It is the intellectual vision she finds very difficult to describe. She can only state that the truths she experienced were of the grandeur of God, and they were like being in her good friend and benefactor's richly endowed room, where she saw many elegant things. But in this case she could not describe them.

St. Teresa is more adept at describing the effects these raptures have on the body. It remains in suspension in the position she was in; it even grows cold and inanimate until the ecstasy is over. But the will is so affected that it remains absorbed, and the intellect is so abstracted that it takes days for it to return to normal. When it does return to normal, it experiences bewilderment, and with a great desire to do penance, but at the same time it feels whatever it does is of little consequence.

When such things occur in public, as they did to her, the soul feels embarrassment and shame, which she says is from a lack of humility. Here in the *Mansions* St. Teresa speaks impersonally, but she relates this same thing in an incident that occurred to her in practically the same words in her autobiography. The Lord consoled her with the words: "Don't be embarrassed, they must either praise me or mutter about you. In whatever of these, you gain" (Mansions VI, 4, 16 and Life XXXI, 13). She glosses over her embarrassment here, but it was so deep (according to her *Vida)* that she even thought of transferring to another strict convent where the distance would make her unknown.

Finally she compares this true rapture with a fake one by its effects. I imagine she is referring to the desire to do penance and the certitude of now belonging to Christ, her Spouse. It would seem that there were many fake raptures taking place not necessarily through malice, but through deception by the Evil one. Today this is a very real temptation among certain charismatics who want desperately to have one of the gifts that others in their group seem to be experiencing. There may be, indeed, some experience, but it is, in this case, most likely, an emotional or psychological one, if not from the devil. The effects are not the same.

The second type of rapture is the subject of this next chapter. She calls it a "flight of the spirit" because it is so swiftly carried off that it seems like the spirit leaves the body. Like St. Paul, who mentions a similar experience to the Corinthians (II, 12:2-4), she was not sure whether it took place in or outside the body. She calls it substantially the same thing as the rapture she was explaining, but different in degree. This conforms with the teaching of St. Thomas on the subject, which he treats of in Question 175 of his *Summa.*

St. Teresa is not concerned with academic niceities so she uses terms like ecstasy, rapture, transport or suspension almost interchangeably. St. Thomas prefers to use this distinction:

"Rapture adds something to ecstasy. For ecstasy means simply a going out of oneself by being placed outside one's proper order; while rapture denotes a certain violence in addition." This, no doubt is what St. Teresa means by a "flight of the spirit." Just as any high ride requires courage at the amusement park, so St. Teresa warns us that much courage is needed to undergo such an experience. Ordinarily the mystics counsel resistance when it comes to prayer experiences, in this case she says any resistance is futile.

This flight of the spirit is often accompanied with levitation, where the body is raised up off the ground, and the person is aware of this. St. Teresa describes in greater detail what she experienced in this way in Chapter 20 of her autobiography. She even had some premonition it was going to happen. On this occasion, she commanded her sisters to hold her down so she wouldn't be a spectacle to the people. They weren't always successful.

We can compare some of these things with what happened to certain Seers of Our Lady, especially those at Garabandal. The children when seeing Our Lady were never in a normal state; their bodies were rigid, but their faces were radiant; sometimes they assumed very awkward positions which defied gravity; they were totally removed from their surroundings in spirit, caught up in another world unaware of time, and weather. Their visions were impressed upon the imagination. We know this because they were able to give specific details of what Our Lady looked like. When St. Teresa says that she saw things with the eyes of the soul, she means imaginary visions, and when she sees with neither the eyes of the body nor of the soul, they are intellectual visions. Things pertaining directly to God or the angels cannot be perceived by the imagination because they are pure spirits. God communicates directly with the intellect, which is a faculty of the soul. We can have knowledge of him and his truths, but be unable to form any image or specific detail of him. When the person returns to his normal self there are then certain telling effects by which one knows that such things were from God, and not the devil or self delusion. St. Teresa enumerates three effects: 1) the grandeur of God; 2) self knowledge and humility by comparison; 3) little esteem for earthly things. In chapter six she will expand on these things. She returns to her comparison of the prayer of union with the stages of a marriage that she mentioned in the Fifth Mansion. She is not completely consistent here, because we are now in the stage of betrothal, but she mentions these effects as being the gifts of her lover, and the rapture as being the meetings between them. In true life these were inferior stages.

As one last consideration, we might ask if what charismatics refer to as being "slain in the spirit" is the same thing as rapture? I would say that the presence of these effects that St. Teresa mentions should determine a rapture's authenticity, together with the great peace and tranquillity it leaves the soul in. The apparitions of Our Lady certainly cause the Seers to go into ecstasy, and they are not always to perfect souls. But most of these Seers admit of a great peace afterward. Many of them wanted to be taken away from this drab world.

This is the subject of chapter six: St. Teresa longed to be taken out of this exile. This is caused from seeing what true reality is like. It becomes a burden to live. This is reflected in her poem, *I die because I do not die.* This in turn causes the soul to have many more raptures. At first, the soul only wants to be left alone; it has a great desire to go off into the desert and be a hermit, and then it desires to convert the world—to share what it has learned. This, of course, is at the basis of the Carmelite vocation. There is no real dichotomy between the contemplative and the active life, seen from this perspective. St. Thérèse was named Patroness of the Missions because of her great desire to bring souls to the love of Christ. St. John Bosco, who was surrounded by children most of his life, also had mystical experiences. Indeed, it is clear that unless one possesses a deep prayer life, his actions many times are ineffective for the Kingdom of God.

St. Teresa also makes the point that these desires are not fleeting, but permanent, and she even counsels those who feel oppressed by not being able to see God, to resist these desires. The early Fathers of the Desert esteemed the gift of tears very highly, and St. Teresa admits that this oppression sometimes causes the flow of tears—an oppression arising from longing to see God. But she is cautious about this, especially among emotional women. Without some resistence one could mistake an emotional release for a divine grace. She distinguishes one from the other again by their effects. Real tears are comforting and tranquillizing, the other disturbing. To her, virtue is more rewarding than tears.

Another aspect of this longing to be with God, which results from these raptures is a strange glee or merriment. This is often translated as jubilation or joy, but because St. Teresa calls this sensation in prayer a sort of nonsense, this type of mirth would be closer to what she says. Actually she is trying to describe a union of faculties, but at the same time the feeling of freedom in both the intellectual part and the senses to enjoy God. This seems like a contradiction. The word she uses is *algarabia* (literally this means Arabic; we would say Greek!). So as we approach these higher states of prayer, the Lord seems to filter his happiness down to our working level, but only after we have everything in line.

This joy is contagious, and the soul wants to spread it abroad. It can no longer contain it in solitude. And this is how we must interpret the perfect joy of St. Francis, whom she mentions here. It is here for the same reason that she speaks of St. Peter of Alcantara, a follower of St. Francis, who was engaged in reforming a group of Franciscans. St. Peter of Alcantara was an extremely ascetical man whom many people regarded as insane, so extreme were his penances. Yet he also had these impulses of happiness, and praised God in public. St. Teresa talks about him at length in chapters 27 and 30 of her *Life*. He was able to clear up many of her doubts in her prayer life. Her comment about people who experience this great joy was if this is madness then "what a blessed madness!"

Indeed Christian joy is a sign of God's presence, and that one's actions are in conformity with the Gospel message. If you will notice as I have, those who are pushing dubious programs, and engaging in dissident activities today are usually very serious to the point of having no sense of humor. I say beware of the intent and fanatical crusader that sees only injustice and oppression around him. A person who cannot laugh at human foibles is very unlikely to experience the transports of joy that St. Teresa is talking about.

Sixth Mansions:
Spiritual Betrothal
Jesus Our Human Companion

(Chapters 7-9)

From the extreme joy that a person experiences after ecstasies St. Teresa now treats of the lingering affliction the soul undergoes over the remembrance of one's past sins. It seems, the assurance of enjoying God forever does not eradicate the grief of having offended the majesty of God. One's former boldness in disobeying God's commands is now sheer affliction. Although St. Teresa says that the fear of hell is no longer present, the soul does fear that if God leaves it to its own strength, it will again offend him. She mentions the Magdalen and St. Peter as examples of this type of affliction; both cried bitter tears of remorse.

We know at one time St. Teresa was given a vision of hell and her possible place in hell if she had not repented. Our Lady in many of her apparitions also allows the seers a glimpse of hell not to scare them, but to impress upon them (and us), the very reality of the consequences of sin. But at this point "loss of heaven and fear of hell" have given way to "most of all because they have offended Thee my God" of the act of contrition.

So she refutes the opinion that now everything is joy. Next she wishes to refute the opinion that now everything is loving, as if one need not meditate on the person of Jesus, but retire into an experience of the Divinity. It is a subject we have treated elsewhere and one she also treats of in chapter 22 of her *Life*. She considers this important because she was for a time misled. In a nutshell, she teaches that one must never abandon the actual corporeal consideration of the man Jesus. There may be times when one is led into spiritual realms of consciousness, but at no time must we consider this humanity of Jesus an impediment to higher prayer. He is after all God's Way to Himself, as he told us. She also has the same thing to say about meditation on the Passion and on the life of the Blessed Virgin or the saints. Today's theologians and liturgists seem to be at variance with this. They even treat Masses to the saints as if they were a deterrent to the worship of Jesus Christ. St. Teresa's comment is: "I cannot imagine what such souls are thinking about!"

She does admit, along with St. John of the Cross, that in

these higher states of prayer meditation becomes difficult and
sometimes impossible, the reason being that once the soul has
become enkindled in love, it no longer needs to think discursive-
ly. But continuous and unimpeded contemplation is impossible
this side of the grave. An ardent love of God comes and goes,
depending on God's favors, but as the saying goes, "God helps
those who help themselves." Until a person has been placed in
perfect contemplation, which is the subject of the Seventh Mansion, he must never consider that the life and passion of Jesus
are below him. St. Teresa dwells on this topic, not only because
she was misled, but also because it was a theological point
greatly discussed, in view of heresies around her. It also had a
direct relation to the liturgical life of the Church, which is
designed to follow the life and sufferings of Jesus. We can easily
appreciate this today where so many liturgists, reflecting the so-
called resurrectional theology would have us view the whole life
of the Church as one of rejoicing in Christ's triumph. This leads
to the attitude that all are saved, and the Mass is but a celebra-
tion of life in the form of a fraternal meal. This ignores the
sacrificial aspect of the Mass.

St. Teresa reasoned that dropping all consideration of the
corporeal aspect of Jesus' life, would eventually lead to a loss of
devotion to the Blessed Sacrament. Another form of this error
today can be grasped from the teaching of certain biblical
scholars who tell us that the Gospels do not narrate the true
history of Christ, but rather give us a symbolic overview of his
message formed by an "impressed" early Christian community.

This statement sums up St. Teresa's attitude, and it would
do us good to ponder it: "He is a very good companion, the
good Jesus for us to withdraw from or his most Holy Mother
and he is very pleased we grieve for his sufferings even though
sometimes we let go of our own happiness and delight (Mansions
VI, 7, 13).

In chapter eight of this mansion St. Teresa enters into a
discussion of another kind of communication with the Lord,
which she calls an intellectual vision. We may well wonder how
a person who describes herself as unlettered can use such precise
terminology. No doubt this comes from her many confessors,
mostly the Dominicans, who knew their Thomistic theology.
In this chapter she speaks in an impersonal way, as she was told
to do in this work, but we can find the same subject-matter in

her *Life*, where she describes what took place to her personally.

She is suddenly aware of the actual presence of the Lord. She knows that he is there, but she does not see him either with her eyes, or her imagination, nor can she describe any detail about him, but her certainty is greater than if he were there in life. She spends much of the chapter trying to explain this and comes up with an analogy like seeing someone in the dark, or rather knowing that someone is there without seeing him. Coupled together with this she intellectually heard a voice say "don't be afraid, it is I!" (Mansions VI, 8, 3). This was what we have described as a substantial locution, which effects what it says.

St. John of the Cross did not go into any great detail about visions, precisely because he knew that St. Teresa had already written about them. But he does help to categorize the different types of communications that one can experience as coming from God. He puts visions, revelations, locutions and spiritual feelings all under intellectual apprehensions. But in the broad sense they can all be called visions of the soul. In this case that St. Teresa is talking about, the visions are spiritual or intellectual because they are not communicated to the intellect through the corporal senses; they are imparted to the intellect without the intervention of either the exterior or the interior bodily senses. This would exclude sense impressions, and the imagination. The knowledge is direct, and therefore it is almost impossible to describe. It would be like trying to describe an intuition.

How can the soul be sure that it is not being deceived by the devil, or that it is a mere illusion caused by some psychological state? St. Teresa gives several beneficial effects: absolute certainty, habitual remembrance of God, peace, continual desire to please God, and although it may experience fear and confusion at times, this is offset by humility and a great love of and surrender to God.

Lastly, St. Teresa counsels those who have been so favored not to talk openly about it. They should reveal such things to their confessor. But she does recognize that certain priests may have a lack of spirituality, and in this case they should discuss it with a learned person. We must recognize in her day that meant someone who knew his theology, and practiced prayer. Unfortunately, today we are encouraged to blab about every experience we have to whomever. There is an abundance of counsellors who are more likely to apply psychology in place of spirituality. It is not a good idea to make profane what is hidden and sacred, especially since it can't be explained adequately anyway.

Let us say just a few more things about visions, especially in view of many claimed visions that have taken place today about the Blessed Virgin. They don't seem to be as rare and unusual in the minds of the faithful as they were once before. And if we can believe at least half of them, these visions don't seem to occur to people who are of an extraordinary holiness. This is a point that St. Teresa also makes: that visions do not indicate necessarily a great holiness, and this also is why St. John of the Cross does not want us to linger over them. Regardless, there are certain visions which do occur to people of an advanced holiness, and these, such as the one described by St. Teresa, cannot be dismissed out of hand.

This intellectual vision of Our Lord is perhaps the least likely to be deluded. St. John of the Cross calls these visions spiritual not because of the object of the vision, but rather because of the means by which it is received. In other words, the light of knowledge comes directly from God, and not from ourselves. As St. Thomas says in his treatment on the prophet's visions, there are four ways we can receive a vision: by the infusion of intelligible light; by the infusion of intelligible species; by the outward presentation of sensible images. St. Teresa's intellectual vision is of the second kind, that is, God gives to the person a vision by infusing intelligible species in the intellect, while it is in a rapture. But even in an intellectual vision we can only attain knowledge of corporal substances, according to St. John. Our minds this side of glory, cannot have direct knowledge of incorporeal substances like our spiritual soul or angels, who are pure spirit. However, there are rare cases when with the help of Divine light, one does get a glimpse of such spiritual substances in what the mystics describe as the substance of the soul. Unless God sustains the life of such an individual, it remains true that "no one can see God and live." We hear this mentioned in the Old Testament, when God approached one of the Patriarchs, even in the form of an angel.

You may object that many of these apparitions of Our Lady began with a vision of an angel. We must understand that these angels have taken many forms—some were children, others strong men. God has presented them to the seers in a form they could recognize, and in a way they could perceive—that is, an imaginative representation. It is interesting though, that in Scripture angels are always presented to us as masculine and with masculine names, unlike what is portrayed on greeting cards. Angels, of course do not have gender, but in presenting them to us as masculine, it is probably symbolic of power, and their role as messengers; one does not send girls with messages.

In chapter 29 of her *Life*, St. Teresa describes the angel which pierced her heart with a fiery dart—*he* was short, very beautiful and his face aflame. It was, according to her, an imaginative vision, unlike other visions she had of angels, which were intellectual. In other words, St. Teresa was one of those rare cases, who had some perception of spiritual substances.

She also seemed to have some type of vision of the soul, which she describes in chapter 40 of her *Life*, where she sees Our Lord in every part of it; this also was an intellectual vision, a rare vision of a spiritual substance, and the basis of this whole work of the *Interior Castle*. You must recall that it is an exposition of the human soul. These visions of incorporeal or spiritual substances are limited and partial, simply because they are beyond our mode of being in this life. All the more should we appreciate the incarnation of the Son of God, where God has presented himself to us in a nature we can grasp. And to want to dump any consideration of Jesus' life and death in our quest for an absolute spirituality, is to ignore the limits of our capabilities in this life.

This brings us to the subject matter of chapter nine, which deals with imaginative visions of Our Lord. These are the third types of visions of St. Thomas, where he says the vision is produced (by God) by the impression or coordination of pictures in the imagination. Since the imagination is a bodily function, which stands between sense and spirit, it is open to workings of the devil. For this reason St. Teresa warns us of his possible influence. But at the same time she recognizes this type of vision as being more in conformity with our nature, and therefore one is able to describe it, and the image is engraven upon the memory. There is one last type of vision which St. Teresa declines to talk about, because she tells us that she never experienced it. This is the last type of vision mentioned by St. Thomas which is formed by the outward presentation of sensible images. This vision is seen with the exterior sense of sight. The vision of Our Lady of Knock was of this kind, and it was seen by many witnessss.

St. Teresa spends the rest of this chapter describing this imaginative vision of Our Lord. First she compares it to the intellectual vision, using the analogy of a precious stone which has curative powers hidden away in a gold vessel. In her day this was a common belief about certain stones. We might be tempted to think this is some quaint magic, but don't we use particles of uranium for radioactive therapy? In any case, suddenly revealing the stone is like an imaginative vision, where we are benefited by its sight. But the sight is with the "inner eye" in this vision; it is brilliant, and comes and goes in a flash, while the soul is in rapture. It can be either of the Lord's humanity when he walked the earth or of his resurrected body. Her reflection is that it is frightening, beautiful, delightful, majestic and far surpassing anything we could conceive of. He is revealed as Lord of heaven and earth. I would like to contrast this conception of Our Lord with the one we are currently instructing our youth. Jesus is and wants to be approachable, but his one Person is both human and divine. We don't do him justice (or ourselves, for that matter) by ignoring one of his natures. We have seen our religion and our youth suffer from a lack of the sacred.

One of the proofs of the authenticity of this vision is its shortness of duration. St. Teresa doubts the soul who says he can gaze at it for a long time, and suggests that the imagination has taken over, especially when that person claims to see everything clearly. One time she tried to see the color of the Lord's eyes, and in so doing she lost the vision. So beware of these visionaries who recount excessive detail and minute instructions.

Authentic visions also occur when least expected, and never concerning things the soul is thinking about. And any tumult or fear from the suddenness of the vision soon gives way to peace and calm. Though the devil can inspire doubts in the soul about visions, and he can even mimic them, a humble soul should not be alarmed, and the soul should report everything to its confessor even when he doesn't understand it; because, as she says, the Lord "is very fond that he who is in his place is treated with the same truth and clarity as himself" (Mansions VI, 9, 12). By this statement St. Teresa not only acknowledges the role of the priest, she understands the authority given to the Church by Christ, when he gave the keys to Peter. But at the same time she recognizes the deficiencies of certain confessors, such as the time when she was counseled to "give the fig!" In chapter eight, verse 3, of her *Book of the Foundations*, she remarks that confessors are more apt to be alarmed with people who speak of visions of God than they are of the harassment of the devil. It is also here that she brings up the subject of a possible vision caused by the devil, and what to do about it. In practically the same words she tells us that a learned confessor told her to make the best of it, by worshiping any image of the Lord, thus turning the devil's ruse into profit. She identified the confessor in the *Foundations*, as Fr. Domingo Bañez, a Dominican and one of the great theologians of his day.

Despite the great benefits and consolations of seeing the Lord in his humanity, St. Teresa now lists the pitfalls of this life of visions, and she lists six reasons against desiring visions: 1) One should never ask God for what he does not deserve; it is a lack of humility. 2) There is a danger of being deceived by the devil. 3) With any desire for a thing the imagination can reproduce it. (St. Teresa can never be accused of indulging in "dream psychology," because here she mentions how people often dream of what they have been thinking about during the day.) 4) It is bold to choose a path that one might not be suited for. 5) One may not have the strength to bear the trials of this way. 6) One gains only by doing God's will. Saul lost his kingship by not obeying exactly what God commanded. She sums this all up by using the Gospel admonition, "To whom much has been given, much will be required." Finally she mentions two people whom she knows—one a man, who prayed to be delivered from extraordinary favors of this kind. It has been conjectured that they were the Saint herself and her confessor at one time, St. John of the Cross. The reason she gives for this is that the ultimate purpose of visions is to increase the virtues. It would be more meritorious to gain them with one's own efforts. This is what St. John counsels: "he who now would want to question God or to desire some vision or revelation, would not only carry out a foolishness but cause an offence against God by not putting his eyes totally on Christ without wanting any other thing or novelty" (Ascent II, 22,5), (P. Crisogono de Jesus, OCD, *Vida y Obras de San Juan de la Cruz*, Madrid, Biblioteca de Autores Cristianos, 1960). But why worry, as St. Teresa says, "I believe that he who desires visions will never be given them" (Mansions VI, 9, 15).

Sixth Mansions:
Spiritual Betrothal
I Die Because I Do Not Die

(Chapters 10-11)

After enumerating all the reasons one should not desire visions and extraordinary spiritual favors in chapter nine, St. Teresa now tells us why the Lord does bestow these things on certain souls. First, to console those who are greatly afflicted, and sometimes as a preparation for affliction, and lastly, simply because the Lord wishes to take some delight in a soul and offer it delight in return.

The only reason she mentions these visions at all, she insists, is to forewarn her sisters that such things can and do take place, and they must not become upset if and when they do. To be overly disturbed by visions would be to play into the hands of the devil, who can cause such doubts and worries, but can't possibly interfere, because these things she mentions are intellectual/spiritual and beyond his grasp.

St. John of the Cross treats of this type of spiritual vision, or apprehension in chapter 25 and the following, of his second book of the *Ascent of Mount Carmel.* He places this under the category of revelation which is the disclosure of some hidden truth, and in this case an intellectual understanding about some truth of God. He goes on to say that this knowledge is so sublime that it can be received only by a person who has arrived at union with God, and that it is God himself who is experienced. Like St. Teresa, he says that it is received in a flash, and the person is incapable of explaining it, except by way of analogy.

In this chapter ten, St. Teresa mentions just two of these sublime truths she experienced. The first is how all things are seen in God, and how he contains them all in himself. She describes this same vision (or revelation) in the last chapter of her autobiography. But in the *Interior Castle* she uses the analogy of God as being an immense palace, wherein dwells everything. In the autobiography he is a huge mirror or diamond. These are the same analogies she uses for the soul in this work. We have to adjust our imaginations here. In the *Interior Castle*, God is in every part of the soul. In this vision, the soul and every part of creation is in God. The mystics were often accused of pantheism because of their insistence that God is everywhere. But in pantheism everything *is* God. In the mystic vision everything is *in* God, but God is still something more.

I would say one of the great errors of this age is that we are taught that it is possible to think of certain things which have no connection with God. Scientific facts are presented to us as not needing God as an explanation. Secular culture has eliminated God from daily life. Youth culture and the entertainment industry now mock God openly because they fail to see him in anything. St. Teresa's vision is in direct contrast to this way of thinking.

In describing this vision in her autobiography, she alludes to God as being in the inmost part of her soul, which, of course, is the basis of the work we are studying. She speaks also of the soul in mortal sin as being covered over with darkness so that it cannot see the Lord, even though he is still there. But now she depicts the soul in God, so that if it sins, it actually sins in the full presence of God and in some way it sins in God himself, thus bringing out the terrible offence against him. We have often been taught that God is such a perfect being, so far above us that we can't hurt him. This is not the experience of St. Teresa. Our sins do hurt and offend him; evil is not just an abstraction. It trespasses against his holiness and purity. We often hear that a person is doing fine as long as he doesn't hurt anybody else; this is how our youth is being trained today. This is a totally false view of sin. As St. Teresa says: "the greatest evil in the world to see is that God our creator suffers so many things from his creatures within his very self" (Mansions VI, 10,3). From this truth, she reminds us how insignificant our offenses are against each other. What an unfathomable lesson God teaches us, at his own expense.

The second vision mentioned in this chapter is that "God is everlasting truth." All truth found in creation is nothing in comparison. For a better and fuller treatment of this vision, we again turn to chapter 40 of her *Life*, vs. 1-4. We must realize that the *Interior Castle* was written in a more impersonal manner than her *Life;* first because it was for a wider audience, and secondly, because St. Teresa was encouraged to be more discreet in view of the Inquisition. It may also be why she left a very important statement about Scripture out of this work. Scripture was a point of great contention in her day; the Council of Trent had decided to maintain the Vulgate as the official version of the Bible. Commentaries in the vernacular were often scrutinized.

In the *Interior Castle*, St. Teresa is content to admonish her sisters to walk in the truth when it comes to self-esteem, and in our works. There is no room here for pride, since all we have is from God. But in her *Life*, she says she became most firmly resolved to carry out the smallest thing contained in Holy Scripture. She also relates the words of this vision, which say, "all the harm which comes to the world is from not knowing the truths of Scripture with plain truth; not one tittle of it will be lacking" (Life XL, 1). This is an important lesson today in view of our great emphasis on Scripture as it is being used in our renewal programs. Too often we are encouraged to approach Scripture from a human point of view, or from its cultural background, as if today it no longer has the same meaning, as when it was written. The eternal inerrancy of Scripture no longer prevails. Our scholars too often use literary forms to refute rather than clarify Scripture. Because we do not grasp or understand what Scripture says, we many times withhold our belief, as if we were the criterion for truth and not Scripture which is God's word. It is interesting that even before St. Teresa was having this revelation, Luther, the father of Protestantism, was busy translating the Scriptures, and promoting the idea of private interpretation on which Protestantism is based.

As she states, St. Teresa thought she already believed in the truth of the Scriptures along with all the faithful. Our Lord said to her, "Ah, daughter, how few love me in truth!" (Life XL, 1). He then explained what this phrase meant: "It is to understand that all is a lie which is not pleasing to me" (Life XL, 1). We conclude, then, that the only way to arrive at truth is to attempt to please God. By this standard, we can see how far off our unbelieving society has wandered. Indeed, when has this consideration been mentioned in any of our programs for renewal?

In the *Interior Castle*, St. Teresa does not mention this locution. Rather she relies on a quotation from the psalms, which says, "every man is a liar." She ends this chapter with one of her most famous quotations. She was wondering why the Lord seemed to promote the virtue of humility, when it occurred to her that the true order of things is that we are nothing and God is truth itself, therefore to be humble is to "walk in truth" (Mansions VI, 10, 7).

In chapter eleven, the last one of the Sixth Mansion, St. Teresa reminds us that she has not forgotten her original analogy of the soul as a little dove or butterfly. She gives us to understand that the soul now approaching the Spiritual Marriage, still has much suffering to endure. All these favors, which St. Peter of Alcantara told her were more apt to be given to women than to men for reasons she purposely omits, have an accumulating effect on the soul, and increase its longing and yearning for God. Perhaps this human desire to love and be loved, is more acute in women than in men. The soul burns interiorly and it only takes the right occasion to set it afire with an experience similar to the one she describes at her transverberation. It is like a blow which wounds the depth of her soul and causes an extreme interior pain. It passes in a flash, but causes a feeling of absence from God. This is succeeded by a vivid knowledge of God. This affliction St. Teresa compares to the sufferings of the souls in purgatory, and draws the conclusion that these sufferings are far worse than those we have to endure on earth. This should give us some incentive to make use of our present sufferings for expiating our sins now instead of later on. What St. Teresa experienced in a flash, could last for a long time in purgatory.

When St. Teresa says, "I saw a person like this" (Mansions VI, 11, 4), she is describing herself. We have her other writings to assure us of this. In the *Interior Castle*, St. Teresa mentions impersonally how the soul is enflamed in these words: "many times it happens through a fleeting thought or through a word one hears about death's delay . . . there comes a blow or as if there might come a fiery arrow" (Mansions VI, 11, 2). In this chapter she later is more specific: "The truth is, that this time completely out of her senses, it came accordingly and severly, only from hearing a word about life not ending" (Mansions VI, 11, 8). (She was in conversation the last day of Eastertide and having been all Easter in such dryness that she hardly realized it was Easter.) Now if we go to her work, the *Spiritual Relations*, (which Fr. Kieran has put under the title *Spiritual Testimonies)* we read in number 15, 1, "All yesterday, I found myself in great loneliness, that if it was not so when I communicated, I had no recollection that it was Easter. Last night when I was with everybody, they sang a little song about how hard it was to suffer living without God" (Relations 15, 1). We can narrow this down even further from the depositions given for St. Teresa's canonization. This incident took place in Salamanca in 1571. The singer was a novice by the name of Isabel of Jesus, and the song goes like this: "Let mine eyes behold Thee, Sweetest Jesu nigh; Let mine eyes behold Thee, And at once I'll die" (Testimony by Isabel de Jesus, quoted by Peers, Works II, p. 327 and Tomas de Jesus, Obras, p. 1524). Under this same sentiment, no doubt, St. Teresa wrote her poem entitled "I die, because I do not die." This is one of the most salient features of this degree of prayer—the desire to die, not out of depression or despondency, but rather out of yearning to be with God. It has reached the state of realization that for all its presence of God, nature still can't deliver in the possession of God. In chapter 20, vs. 13 of her *Life*, she says, "I really think sometimes, the Lord must be served if it continues as now, that it would end up with ending my life."

As I mentioned, this yearning is coupled with intense pain, not primarily of the body, but of the soul. The attacks last no longer than three or four hours. It is her opinion that if they lasted longer, it would indeed result in the death of the body. The body does not go unscathed either. One's pulse almost stops, and the body grows cold and rigid. Even the next day St. Teresa felt pain in her body as if her bones were disjointed. The natural desire of the body and the soul to remain together is another source of anguish. It "feels a strange loneliness" (Mansions VI, 11, 5), because it realizes that no creature on earth can give it comfort.

She makes two reflections on this suffering. One is the likeness of the sufferings of hell. She emphasizes how much greater the sufferings of a spiritual nature are than those of the body. But a soul in this life and in this prayer is resigned and even content to endure suffering for God, but those of hell are not, and they cannot look forward to a time when relief will come. Finally St. Teresa tells us why God afflicts these souls in this manner. He wants us to "be more conscious of how much we owe him" (Mansions VI, 11, 7), by giving us the hope of being free of our sins.

The other reflection concerns the Blessed Virgin. It comes from one of her spiritual testimonies where she tries to compare the transfixing of her soul with that of the Blessed Virgin. It was revealed to her that Our Risen Lord first visited his Mother because of the great pain she experienced which "so absorbed and transpierced her soul that she did not even return to herself to rejoice in that joy" (Relations XV). She concludes that her's was nothing in comparison.

There are at least three benefits for having suffered this experience: 1) there is little fear of further trials. In other words nothing could be worse; 2) greater contempt for the world; it is unable to help it; and 3) greater fear of offending the Lord; it realizes the pains of hell.

There are two things in this experience which seem to put a soul in danger of death. The first is the actual pain and anguish; the second is the overwhelming joy and delight. This latter may at first seem strange, since St. Teresa hasn't given us a very positive or optimistic view of this experience in this chapter. She has one little sentence which can give us a happier impression. Talking about a remedy for the pain, she says, "the Lord himself takes it away, which is almost always the case, with a great rapture or some vision where the true Consoler comforts and strengthens, so that it wants to live all that is his will" (Mansions VI, 11, 9). She repeats this in her *Relations* (5, 19) where she says, "those great impulses are almost never taken away except with a rapture and the great gift of the Lord where he comforts the soul and incites it to live for him."

All this might be enough to deter people from advancing in prayer if we did not appreciate the necessity of the cross in the message of Jesus. Thus St. Teresa counsels courage and warns the person who seeks spiritual delights, visions and other favors, will also get a giant's share of the cross as well as joys.

Seventh Mansions: Spiritual Marriage
Vision of the Trinity

(Chapters 1-2)

Even though St. Teresa mentions a sort of open door between these last two mansions, in the Sixth Mansion, she is more intent on telling us about the continuing afflictions and the trials of these higher states of prayer. But in this last mansion in which occurs the Spiritual Marriage between the soul and God, she concentrates on the interior state of the soul. To her was given the ability of explaining what takes place. She can only give impressions and intuitions because these things are beyond human experience. But in these there is present a certitude of Faith.

She begins this mansion with the same reflection she wrote in the first chapter of this whole book: that we do not appreciate the nature of our own souls as images of God. She at first hesitates to say more about this matter, mainly because she was aware of how unworthy she is to have arrived at this state, and how presumptuous people would feel she was for daring to speak of such matters. But then she felt she owed it to those who might follow her. Besides, she reasoned that she would be dead by the time it was read. She was not altogether incorrect in assuming this. She gave the finished manuscript to her Provincial, who first entrusted it to the Prioress of the Carmelites in Seville, and the year she died, 1582, he gave it to a wealthy benefactor. The rest of the story is that it found its way back to the convent of Seville, when this benefactor's daughter entered that convent in 1618.

In considering the soul, St. Teresa wants us to know that it is clothed in light, except when it is in mortal sin. Here she includes a profitable meditation on those in mortal sin. According to her *Spiritual Testimonies* (no. 13) she failed to profit from all the graces God had given her since she was a child, yet he forgave her and raised her now to this high estate. From this she concluded that no one is hopeless in God's eyes. All the more reason, she exhorts her sisters, to pray for those in mortal sin. After this reflection on our human fraility, St. Teresa resumes the subject matter. In the Castle God has his own private room, and in the Seventh Mansion God now brings the soul into this room with him. She acknowledges that during a rapture or during prayer of union which she has previously discussed, God unites the soul with himself, but here at the Spiritual Marriage, the soul is drawn even deeper into its center *(el mas profundo centro del alma)*. This also is a mysterious term used by St. John of the Cross, and the German mystics before him. In the former types of union, that is, such as a rapture, the faculties are blinded, and lost, but in this union of the Spiritual Marriage, the soul has some perception of what is taking place. She describes it as a certain representative of the truth in which the three Persons of the Blessed Trinity are revealed as one substance, yet distinct. St. John of the Cross treats of this in the *Ascent*, chapter 24, which he calls a revelation of naked truths, where God reveals himself to the substance of the soul. What we hold by Faith, the soul grasps with certitude. The soul now perceives the three Divine Persons, "some place deep within itself." Unlike before, the recipient of this favor is not absorbed by God to the degree that it is abstracted from its surroundings. It is now more conscious of things pertaining to the service of God, and more careful not to offend God in anything. There is a constant awareness of God's presence, sometimes more vividly than others, but never more vivid than the first time this union takes place.

By all this, we can see that all the extraordinary things that took place before, such as raptures, ecstasies, visions, locutions, etc., were due more to the imperfection of the soul than its perfection. In other words, the perfect soul, being more in tune with God, is able to sustain God's presence because it is living more in the spirit than in the material-sense life it formerly maintained.

Nor can we judge spiritual matters from a human or even rational perspective. Concerning this habitual experience of the Three Divine Persons in her soul, St. Teresa wondered how this could be, since she was accustomed to experience only the person of Jesus. She recounts this in her *Relations*, 18. Our Lord intervened, telling her that she was mistaken in thinking of things of the soul through a comparison with corporeal things, "that I should know that these were very different and that the soul was capable of great fruition."

Taking this into consideration, then, we have some understanding of St. Teresa's experience that the soul and the spirit seem to be different. She also experiences a difference between the soul and its faculties, yet we know rationally they are all one. Her spiritual perception is more acute, and once, she says, she complained to the Lord like Martha did about Mary. While she was busy about many things, and experiencing trials, she felt envious about that part of her soul that was enjoying the Lord's presence. I suppose psychologists would have a field day in describing how schitzoid her personality was! On the purely natural level we have some inkling of this when we talk to ourselves, as if we were two and not one person.

The two principle benefits of this habitual presence of the Lord are the loss of fear of extraordinary favors, in whatever way they may be granted, and a great help in the advancement of perfection. The essential part of her soul, she felt, never left that room where the Lord dwells, thus the difference between Spiritual Betrothal and Marriage.

In the second chapter of this Seventh Mansion, St. Teresa describes as best she can what takes place at the moment of this Spiritual Marriage; and in this chapter she elaborates on many of the things she has already mentioned in the first. Fortunately, she adds other details in her various *Spiritual Relations.* This great favor is initiated by an imaginative vision of the Lord's Sacred Humanity. She discreetly puts this account in the second person. She tells us that she had just received communion, when the Lord appeared to her "in the form of great splendor, beauty and majesty as he was after being resurrected" (Mansions VII, 2, 1). She fills this out in *Relation* 35. It was the second year of her prioress-ship at the Incarnation, and it occurred on the octave day of the feast of St. Martin (November 18). The priest who gave her communion was St. John of the Cross. Moreover, she suspected that by breaking the host for another sister, and giving her only half, he was trying to mortify her, because she had previously told him she liked large hosts. (The Carmelites to this day take large hosts for communion.) In this second chapter she continues, that the Lord told her it was "now time that she take his things for hers and he would take care of hers" (Mansions VII, 2, 1). She also said that he spoke other words. These words are recounted in the aforementioned *Relations.* It seems the Lord took this occasion to demonstrate his concern for her. He said, "Don't fear daughter, for no one will be a part of keeping you from me" (Relations 35). Here we have the lesson that many times God uses human events to bestow his favors upon us. Then in this imaginative vision Christ extended his right hand and said, "Look at this nail which is the sign that you will be my bride from today on. Until now you have not merited this, from here on, not only will you look to my honor as Creator, King and your God, but also as my true Spouse. My honor is yours and yours is mine" (Relation 35).

There are at least two significant things about this vision: first it was an imaginative vision, that is, there was some representation in the imagination, almost as if to say that Christ was after all a man, who lives and can be seen. Secondly, the vision occurred in the depths of her soul, not outside, as if to confirm the fact that Christ now lives within us. And the vision of the Trinity also came from within after the vision of Christ's humanity. This points to the fact that Christ is, after all, the revelation of the Trinity; it is through him that we know the Trinity. He remains the Way for all humanity. The vision of Christ's humanity, although from the depth of the soul was an imaginative one, but the subsequent one, which followed immediately of the Blessed Trinity was an intellectual one. The great difference of this intellectual vision from others of the Lord was that it, too, came from the center of her soul. Oddly the startling thing about this event was the appearance of Our Lord to her in an imaginative vision, because she was not accustomed to see him in this way. Moreover the depth of the intellectual vision of the Trinity made her realize that God's spirit and hers were joined. The mystics, following St. Paul speak of this union in terms of the consummation which takes place in human marriage, yet only by analogy. In writing about this St. Teresa was careful not to give the wrong impression. She changed one sentence by crossing out the wording and adding something more discreet. In place of "those who have consummated matrimony," she puts, "as it is between two spouses, those who no longer can be separated" (Mansions VII, 2, 2—see note by P. Tomas). She does this twice in this chapter. And she explains, "It is understood that here there is no recollection of the body than if the soul were not in it . . ." (Mansions VII, 2, 3).

St. Teresa remembers her initial analogy of the silkworm and the butterfly. It is here that the butterfly dies; it is here too that the soul dies to itself and is transformed into another Christ. She quotes St. Paul's famous passage from Phillipians, "for me to live is Christ, and to die is gain." And at various times she feels that God is indeed the life of her soul. She refers again and again to the truth of Scripture, especially the Gospel of St. John where the Lord promises to come to those who keep his commandments, where he and the Father and the Holy Spirit will make their abode with them. Another thing that St. Teresa stresses is the peace the soul remains in. Although the faculties and the senses can still have their ups and downs, the soul in its inmost center is at peace.

At this point we may well ask, that since the soul has reached union with God, it now has nothing more to fear; its salvation is assured. This was the teaching of the Alumbrados or the Quietists of her day, and it was something which disturbed the Inquisition. But St. Teresa goes on to assure us that this is not her meaning at all. The soul is secure as long as the Lord sustains it in grace, and as long as the soul does not offend God. In other words, the soul is still free to backslide. Moreover, she tells us that in this state, the soul is even more careful about committing the slightest offence, and has even greater misgivings about its past sins than before. Its great desire is to do the Lord some service and regrets that it can do no more. I imagine what she says about the lack of health and strength which sometimes renders a soul incapable of doing greater penances refers to her own condition.

In the last paragraph of this chapter, St. Teresa comes back to her original analogy of the Castle. She insists that no poison-our creatures (sins) or other disturbances, even though they can be heard in the other mansions (the soul is not oblivious to what is going on around it) can enter this mansion of the King. The passions cannot enter it. This means that the passions are under control and do not affect the tranquility of the soul. Does this mean that the joy, hope, sorrow and fear, mentioned by St. John, cannot be felt in this mansion? It probably means that they have all been referred to God. In any case, St. Teresa leaves no doubt that the soul which has reached this state by the grace of God, is at peace both with itself and with its Creator.

Seventh Mansions:
Spiritual Marriage
Life in God is No Time To Rest

Chapters 3-4)

These last chapters of the *Interior Castle* treat of the effects of this high state of prayer, and its purpose, in the mind of St. Teresa. Spiritual Marriage signifies not only a perfect state of prayer, but a perfect state of being, insofar as one can attain this in this life. So naturally it is of interest to us (as it was to St. Teresa) how this soul differs from its former imperfect life. It is not always easy to detect holiness in a person, especially by one who has no desire for it. But it is not for these that St. Teresa writes.

The first effect and the second are enumerated; there are others which can be distinguished from the text. Fr. Thomas of Jesus in his revised *Works (Obras) of St. Teresa* gives us the rest in a footnote. Altogether there are six effects enumerated in this chapter. In order, they are: 1) forgetfulness of self, 2) the desire to suffer, 3) a great interior joy in persecution, 4) a great desire to serve God and not to die, 5) detachment from everything, 6) no fear of the devil's disembling.

Let us see what St. Teresa means by each of these effects: the first one is forgetfulness of self. It is here that her simile of the butterfly dies; it is here that the marriage is consummated, so that the lover and the beloved become one; it is here that the soul and God are united, so that the soul all but loses its identity. It stands to reason that she experiences little care for anything except what relates as to God. Heaven, life or honor don't seem to have any more grasp on her desires. But this is not the same as a profound indifference towards all things, as many experience in the beginning stages of prayer. It means instead, that she has ordered all things towards God. Unlike former stages, too, she does not walk around in an ecstatic stupor. Some people have the idea that high stages of prayer are synonymous with levitation and abstraction from one's surroundings. On the contrary, one seems to be better grounded than before, and one goes around with attention to his daily tasks, and if the soul sees any particular thing as more worthy of giving honor and glory to God, its energy is greater, and its grief is that it can do no more. The only analogy I can make is that of the artist engaged in his work; he is lost to himself, and so preoccupied that all other considerations are peripheral.

The second effect is the desire to suffer, or rather the willingness to suffer. On the human plane most people are unwilling to experience the least discomfort, and this reluctance itself causes greater pain than is present. Of course, meaningless pain is to be avoided. We must realize that the suffering is in God's plan or else he would not have had his Son suffer and die on a cross. You may think that the person who actually enjoys suffering is mentally ill or a first degree stoic, but if that person can come to understand suffering in the light of salvation, and in the light of imitating God's Son, then a spiritual joy in it is conceivable, and even desireable. St. Teresa had many physical pains in her life, but these are not what she is referring to in this chapter. She specifically mentions suffering in the context of persecution, and many times it is a persecution from one's friends and not one's enemies. In her case, it came from the authorities over her, her own sisters, and her priest confessors, usually because they did not understand her way of prayer. She conceived of a great love for her Father Provincial, Fr. Gracian, whom she held in higher esteem than he deserved. And in her letters she reveals her disappointment in some of his actions, which went contrary to her advice. Well-meaning people can be a great source of pain, but seen from the angle of God's providence the irritation they cause us can be a source of grace. But the soul in this state goes one step further; it not only puts up with its persecutors, it prays for them and even loves them, and goes out of its way to help them. Is this not what Jesus did for us on the cross? This love and joy in persecution is the third effect mentioned by St. Teresa. The fourth is the desire to serve God in this life. Formerly, the soul went through a period when it suffered greatly because it could not die and be with its Lord. This may still happen occasionally, but for the most part, it is indifferent to living or dying, and it sees all that must be accomplished for the Lord, to gain souls for the Kingdom. It now wants to offer its suffering for the Crucified, and to die would be a consolation; it has moved from the desire for consolation to the desire for suffering. And in this state, the soul no longer fears death. A soul that does not fear suffering or pain has relieved itself also of all fear of death. Indeed this is no small comfort, since man's primary drive is to maintain life. In a sense the soul now knows what true life is, and it has to a limited degree attained that life with God. In this we get some small glimpse of the Assumption of the Blessed Virgin Mary. Her life while on earth was a continuous union with her Lord, so it could not have been a traumatic separation, when she came into her glory. Indeed, the body which held her Lord, could not find a fitting place to rest this side of heaven.

In paragraph eight St. Teresa makes a very startling statement about Jesus. She says, "His life was nothing but a continual torment" (Mansions VII, 3, 2). I recently read in the question and answer series in a Catholic paper this question: "Was Jesus fun to be with?" The inanity of the question was enough to have been ignored, and it is a commentary on the present state of catechetics. According to St. Teresa, in this state of prayer, the Lord makes the soul the same as he. But at the same time the soul has no aridities or interior trials. Those, after all, were the result of some disorder between body and soul.

Detachment from everything is the sixth effect. This would stand to reason since in possessing God interiorly, the soul has no need or desire for anything else. It wants only to be alone in solitude or busy helping some soul.

Most of St. Teresa's phenomena have ceased except for the same "impulses" she mentioned in chapter two of the Sixth Mansion. These are experienced when the soul is distracted, and seem to come from deep within the soul, except now they do not come like a thunder-clap, but in a gentle manner. So we must realize that the soul even in the highest state can be distracted by the world. The gentle manner of the impulse would indicate the greater detachment of the soul.

The last mentioned effect of this state of prayer is the lack of fear about the devil's influence. The interior of the soul is off limits to the devil, and what comes from God is experienced as a direct communication—not even the understanding or the desiring of the soul has any influence. All takes place in silence; there is no ecstasy, but the faculties seem to be there as dumbfounded spectators. The soul never or rarely experiences the raptures it had before. Music, sermons, devotional objects do not "turn it on" as before. Public manifestations are taken away and the soul does not have to fear the unexpected taking place.

Even though the soul has found its repose, it is by no means complacent; it fears that all could be lost if it is not constantly on its guard. They have a greater knowledge of their own misery and weakness, and their sins and faults are more serious to them. But they find peace in the mercy of God. The cross they bear, and their fears do not allow them to lose their peace. In general they cannot help but be optimistic.

In this last chapter, St. Teresa now tells us that even the Spiritual Marriage does not deliver one from the natural state of this life. There are times of great disturbance and these effects are not present. However, the soul has gained enough determination not to be completely thrown off its course. She tells us that the Lord perhaps wants the soul always to be humble and not let these favors make it feel more important. These periods of unrest are usually the result of some external event and they last but a day or two.

The soul at this stage is still capable of imperfections and even venial sins which are inadvertent. It feels and is free from mortal sins, but she adds, not immune from them. The soul is not exactly confirmed in grace, according to her. This difference between her and St. John of the Cross, who leads us to believe that the soul in union with God is confirmed in grace, is perhaps due to her sceptical attitude toward her own capabilities. She mentions Solomon, who in spite of all the gifts he had received, fell into disfavor before the Lord. She also counsels the one who feels the safest, should also have the most fear of the Lord. This attitude is in contrast to the Alumbrados of her day, who taught that the perfect were now free to do as they pleased.

In paragraph four of this chapter St. Teresa reveals what she thinks is the whole purpose of God's favors, and his guidance of the soul to this point. She says, "His Majesty can do no greater thing for us than to give us a life which is imitating that which his so-much-beloved Son lived" (Mansions VII, 4, 4). The favors, mind you, are specifically given to imitate the Lord's great sufferings. To make this point, she mentions the sufferings endured by the Lord's Mother, the Apostles, especially Saints Peter and Paul, and later on by the Magdalen.

As if to counter the possible attitude that this state now allows us to rest secure, she tells her sisters not to be worrying about self, or honors, or resting; they should look for ways to please God. The reason for prayer is the love of God, and from this will flow good works. She repeats the word "works" *(obras)* twice in this sentence (Mansions VII, 4, 6). There is nothing Lutheran about St. Teresa! Resolutions and good intentions, even coming from prayer are nothing if they are not put into practice. Her remedy for detachment lies in Jesus crucified. She makes a special effort to stress this one thing: "Fix your eyes on the Crucified and all of it will be for you, but little" (Mansions VII, 4, 8). And as if she were running down prayer itself, she says we cannot please God by words alone. For her, the truly spiritual person is more than being prayerful, it consists of the attitude of complete surrender to God, as a slave, which requires great humility. Humility she considers the foundation of the whole *Interior Castle.* Prayer and contemplation, as important as they are, unless they lead to the practice of virtue, will not serve to increase our holiness. The soul, now that it understands the benefit of great trials, does not retire from bodily works, it increases them and it appreciates the strength it gains from living with companions who are engaged in the same fight. Greater strength comes to the spirit, too, in its intimate contact with the Lord of the Castle, which causes it to desire more bodily strength than it has in doing penance. So it suffers in not being able to do more. It is here that she enters into a discussion of Mary and Martha, declaring that the two must go hand in hand. This attests to the truth that true prayer is not contrary to active works, but rather inspires one to the active apostolate, and when this is not possible, as was the case of St. Thérèse, to a greater desire to share the benefits of her prayer. On the other hand, it is a great temptation to want to share your charity with the world, especially someone far off, while neglecting to practice that same charity to those immediately around you. I have seen this happen so often in community, where some members have gained a large following on the outside, and they have done some commendable things for others, while causing only dissension and ill-feeling among their own brethren. They may place the blame on their community, because of some personality or other, but perhaps they have not really learned who their neighbor is, and failed to put into practice the virtues, where it would have been more meritorious.

Our work here on earth does not consist of great things

(the Lord does not need us for that), it consists rather in doing all with great love. Love and sacrifice go together, and when these are united with that sacrifice of Jesus on the cross, they become of infinite value. With a prayer for a remembrance, St. Teresa ends this work of the *Interior Castle*. Contrary to what we might expect in these last chapters of this high state of prayer, St. Teresa seems to bring us back to earth in her admonition for the practice of virtue. We get a glimpse of real holiness from her account, as not being so high-flown and untouchable as we could expect. It is a picture of a man who has been delivered from original sin. This man doesn't differ so much from us sinners, except that this man is well-ordered, calm, humble and truthful. There is no trace of selfishness and he has God as his companion. In a word, this man/woman resembles Christ, and the Castle is all his.

St. Teresa adds a prologue to this finished work, in which she commends the reading of it to her sisters for whom it was primarily written. With tongue in cheek she tells them they can enter the Castle and walk about any time they wish without getting permission from their superior. This is an off-handed reference to the rules of their convents, which forbade the sisters to go to chapel without permission. She makes it clear that her seven mansions are an arbitrary number; there can be many more. She asks them to pray for an increase in membership in the Church, for light for the Protestants, pardon for her sins, and deliverance from purgatory. The work was begun reluctantly on June 2, 1577 at the original convent of San Jose in Avila, and concluded there on the 9th of November 1577—a little less than six months.

PART II

DOCTRINAL STUDIES

Man, The Image of God

One day in Seville in the year 1575, St. Teresa experienced a type of vision unlike "other visions," she said, "for it reinforces faith." It was a vision concerning the presence of God in her soul. "I was astonished," she continues, "to see so much majesty in such a lowly thing as my soul." Then she heard these words: "It is not lowly, daughter, for it is made in my image" (Relations, 54).

Thus St. Teresa adds her name to the long list of Christian philosophers, theologians and saints who considered this basic but still obscure concept concerning the relationship between God and man. Basic, because it is perhaps the oldest expression of this relationship found in revelation. It was used in no later than the 26th verse of the first chapter of Genesis, where the sacred author portrays a somewhat anthropomorphic concept of the Creator deliberating upon the creation of man. "And he said: Let us make man to our image and likeness . . . and God created man to his own image; to the images of God he created him . . ." Obscure, because in these words are contained the doctrine, not only of man's nature, which is a peculiar blending of the human and the divine, but also of God's nature, which of necessity will always remain shrouded in impenetrable mystery.

It will always remain a testimony to the integrity of the Hebrew copyists and to the enduring guidance of the Holy Spirit that this line of Scripture was not changed. What could the use of the plural form for God have meant to a monotheistic people such as the Jews? And yet they never changed the words *let us*—to *let me*. Some exegetes have seen in this use of the plural form a foreshadowing of the Christian revelation of the Trinitarian nature of the Creator. We might add, since it is linked in context in this particular passage with man, there would seem to be at least a hint of the divine indwelling of the Trinity in the soul of man.

There was much discussion over this cryptic phrase among the earlier theologians, especially among the Doctors of the

Eastern Church. Irenaeus, for instance, wanted to distinguish between the meaning of the words *image* and *likeness*. St. Cyril of Alexandria, who wrote more extensively on the subject, considers the two ideas synonymous. The great discussion, however, centered about the actual meaning of the phrase *image of God*.

How is man the image of God? In what does this image consist? Let us use an analogy. When a person looks into a mirror, he sees his image staring back at him. He knows, of course, that this image is not the same as his physical self, but at the same time, for all appearances, there is an exact reproduction of himself, which in a more vulgar vein might be called the "spitting image" of him. Having accepted the fact of our being in the image of God from revelation, our next step is to determine how this can be. There obviously must be something in the mirror itself which enables it to reflect the person looking into it. It must contain certain properties which give it the power to reflect. Glass seems to be the most apt subject for reflecting, but anything shiny will do the same thing, such as water or metal. So it is not so much in the physical, external surface. Some metals will not reflect, some glass we can only see through. Applying our analogy to man, both man and animals have similar physical properties, yet never has it been said that an animal is made to the image of God. There is something required in the metal or glass in order to make it a true mirror. It must be backed with some solid surface, such as quicksilver in the case of glass. So in man there must be a property which enables him to be receptive to reflect God and thus be an image of God.

St. Augustine found it in man's lordship or his dominion over created things. But this does not solve our problem, it only prolongs it. There must be something which gives man this dominion over created things. Something in man's very nature.

St. Cyril and St. Thomas (and from the opening quotation of this article, it would seem) St. Teresa ascribe to the *soul* the ability to be the image of God. In the words of St. Thomas:

> "Man is said to be after the image of God not as regards his body, but as regards that whereby he excels other animals. Hence when it is said 'Let us make man to our image and likeness,' it is added, 'And let him have dominion over the fishes of the sea.' Now man excels all animals by reason and intelligence (properties of the

soul); hence it is according to his intelligence and reason, which are incorporeal, that man is said to be according to the image of God" (Summa Theol. Ia IIae, q.3, a.2, ad obj.2).

But neither St. Thomas nor St. Teresa stop here in their consideration of the image. Only when the intellect and the will have God as the object do they fulfill the function for which they were made. "Since man is said to be to the image of God by reason of his intellectual nature he is the most perfectly like God according to that in which he can best imitate God in his intellectual nature. Now the intellectual nature imitates God chiefly in this, that God understands and loves himself" (Summa Theol. Ia IIae, q.90, a.4). Moreover, only when our thoughts are of God or contain God, and our wills attached to God does our soul find fulfillment. As St. Augustine says in his *Confessions;* "We were made for Thee, O Lord, and our hearts will not rest until they rest in Thee." But this is not to say only when we think of God directly are we images of God. And this is where our analogy limps. Our image is found in the mirror only when we stand before it. Whereas, our souls mirror Almighty God *always*, because he is always before them, or more properly, they are always before God. He is so all-pervading that we cannot escape him. Such was the experience of St. Teresa when she says: "Once I learned how the Lord was in all things and how he was in the soul and the comparison came to me of a sponge which absorbs water in itself" (Relations, 45).

It is by reason of her soul, then, that St. Teresa realized God was with her in a special manner, even though he was present to all creation. This presence of God in the soul must be distinguished from his presence in all creation. Moreover, St. Teresa sees an intimate connection between the presence of God and the image.

In the vision we mentioned at the beginning of this chapter, St. Teresa "reinforced with faith" and also with the knowledge of her Dominican confessor, found she "could not doubt that the Trinity is by presence and by power and essence in our souls." "It is a thing of the greatest benefit to understand this truth." "I also learned some things about the cause by which God delights in souls more than in other creatures, things so delicate that although the intellect quickly grasps them, I didn't know how to explain them" (Relations 54).

She takes this reflection up again some two years later as she hurriedly begins her most famous work, the *Interior Castle:*

> "Truly our intellects must hardly come to a comprehension of it, acute as they may be, anyhow they cannot reach an understanding of God for he himself says that he created us in his image and likeness. For if this is so, as it is, there is no use in tiring ourselves in wanting to comprehend the beauty of this Castle, for (the Castle) is a creature, it is enough for his Majesty to say that it is made in his image in order that we can hardly understand the great dignity and beauty of the soul" (Mansions I, 2).

Although she could not adequately explain this image of God, St. Teresa was given brief glimpses into this mystery. When she came to write the *Interior Castle*, it was on this basic doctrine that she built her whole conception of the Mansions. Accordingly as a soul progresses in prayer this image becomes more manifest to that soul.

She saw clearly in the beginning that at no time was this image absent—not even to a person in a state of sin. She notes:

> "Let us consider here that the spring and that resplendent sun which is in the center of the soul does not lose its splendor and beauty which is always within it, and nothing can take away its beauty. But if over a crystal which is in the sun one should place a very black cloth, surely, although the sun shines on it, its brightness will have no action on the crystal" (Mansions I, 2, 3).

In this St. Teresa is right in line with St. Thomas, who treats not only of the sinner, but even of those bereft of reason. He states: "Whether this image of God be so obsolete, as it were clouded, as almost to amount to nothing as in those who have not the use of reason, or obscured and disfigured as in sinners, or clear and beautiful as in the just, the image of God abides ever in the soul" (Summa Theol. Ia Iae, a.93, a.8, ad obj. 3).

In another place St. Teresa describes the soul in mortal sin as a mirror which is covered "with a great haze and remains very black, thus it cannot image or see this Lord even though he is always present giving us our being" (Life XL, 5). The sinner suffers a terrible lack of vision, but the heretic is left with even more devasting consequences, according to her analogy, for "with heretics it is as if the mirror were broken which is worse than obscured" (Life LX, 5).

This analogy of the mirror which St. Teresa mentions in her life is interesting, and it compares with her later analogy of the diamond in the *Interior Castle*. Perhaps if she were alive today she would use the analogy of a glass house in order to depict the soul. The most important thing about these analogies is the presence of Our Lord in the very center. This seems to be consonant with the doctrine of divine grace which (without going too deeply into theology) raises man to a new level of living. Grace does more than add something to the soul; it transforms the soul and lifts it to a supernatural state—a life with God. This is how St. Teresa explains her soul in a state of grace:

"Suddenly my soul was recollected and it seemed to me to be bright all over like a mirror, without having back nor sides nor top or bottom that was not all bright and in the center of it was pictured Christ, Our Lord, as I usually see him. It appeared I saw him in all parts of my soul, clear as in a mirror and also this mirror, I don't know how, was all engraven in the Lord himself through a communication that I don't know how to describe, but very loving" (Life LX, 5).

St. Teresa is mainly interested in the image of God in man according to grace. St. Thomas says:

"The image of God is in man in three ways. First, inasmuch as man possesses a natural aptitude for understanding and loving God; and this aptitude consists in the very nature of the mind, which is common to all men. Secondly, inasmuch as man actually or habitually knows and loves God, though imperfectly and this image consists in the conformity of grace. Thirdly, inasmuch as man knows and loves God perfectly; and this image consists in the likeness of glory" (Summa Theol. Ia IIae, q.93, a.4).

And since this conformity of grace increases with the influx of grace, then the image of God in man would seem to become increasingly more distinct and predominant. It is this that St. Teresa so aptly describes in her exposition of the seven mansions. God lives in all creation because it needs him to sustain it. God lives in all men in a more distinct manner because they image him in their natural make-up. God lives in the souls of the just in a closer fashion and takes his delight in them because they are most like him in their actions. This, St. Teresa readily recognizes in these words: "the soul of the just man is no other thing but a paradise where he says he takes his pleasure" (Mansions I, 1, 1). Those souls who reach the heights of sanctity are given the clearest vision of God within their own souls. St. Teresa prefaces the Seventh Mansion with a reminder: "for each of us has one (a soul) except that as we do not prize them as a creature made in the image of God deserves, thus we do not understand the great secrets that are in them" (Mansions VII, 1, 1). "Now our good God wants to remove the scales from our eyes that it may see and understand something of the mercy that he gives it" (Mansions VII, 1, 6).

Having reached the highest degree of prayer and having attained mastery over its faults, the soul according to St. Teresa:

> ". . . is put in that mansion by an intellectual vision; by a certain way of revelation, of the truth the Most Holy Trinity is revealed to the soul, all three persons, with an enkindling that just comes to its spirit like a cloud of the greatest clarity, and these distinct Persons by an admirable knowledge which is given, the soul understands with the greatest truth to be all three Persons one substance and one power and one knowledge and only one God; In like manner what we know through faith, there the soul understands, we can say by sight, although it is not seen with the eyes of the body nor of the soul because it is not an imaginary vision. Here all three Persons commune with it and speak to it and make it understand those words which the Gospel says that the Lord said He and the Father and the Holy Spirit would come to dwell with the soul who loves him and keeps his commandments" (Mansions VII, 1, 6).

St. Teresa has reached the ultimate stage of interiorization and she declares: "one can say no more than that in so far as one can understand, the soul (rather I say the spirit of this soul) is made one thing with God" (Mansions VII, 2, 6). "This one understands better, as time goes on, through its effects" (Mansions VII, 2, 6). In this state the soul experiences only peace and tranquillity, "the passions are already conquered" (Mansions VII, 2, 11). And there is found great joy in suffering.

St. Teresa places all confidence in the words of Christ which promise his presence and she blames us for not preparing ourselves if we do not come to this realization of his presence. "And how we all could understand it, if it were not through our own fault, for the words of Jesus Christ, our King and Lord, cannot fail. But as we fail in not disposing ourselves and wander from all that can embarrass this light" (Mansions VII, 2, 8).

At this point she indicates the blending of our image into the Godhead in so far as that is possible, when she wisely says: "we do not see ourselves in this mirror which we contemplate where our image is engraven" (Mansions VII, 28). So it seems God is in us according to his presence through an image and our image at the same time is found to be engraven upon God.

In the ensuing years St. Teresa learned much about this presence of God in her soul, especially of the one God and three Persons. It was a progressive realization. In the year 1571, she experienced a vision which confused her. She couldn't understand how Jesus could dwell in her soul along with the Blessed Trinity, even though she knew all were one God. She says:

"... The Lord told me today as I was thinking about this; that I was wrong in imagining things of the soul with the image of those of the body, that I should understand that they were very different and that the soul was capable of great joy. It seemed it was pictured to me as when a sponge is united and absorbs water; thus it seemed my soul which was filled with that divinity and in a certain way rejoiced within itself and possessed the three Persons" (Relations, 18).

In order to give St. Teresa the proper perspective of his presence, Our Lord said to her: "Don't exert yourself to have me enclosed within you, but enclose yourself within me" (Relations, 18). "It seemed that within my soul that these three Persons were there and I saw them—they made themselves known to all created things, not failing nor lacking to be with me" (Relations, 18).

In other words, we must not think that this image consists in reflecting the human characteristics of Jesus Christ alone. Our souls must reflect the divine life of Jesus as well as the human life. This life is Trinitarian in nature. Our souls are images of the whole Trinity. After a certain vision, Teresa declares: "I have remained from here on unable to think of any of the three Divine Persons without realizing that all are three" (Relations, 47). But at the same time she realized the important role of the Incarnation or the Humanity of Christ, and before attaining such exalted knowledge of the Trinitarian relationships, St. Teresa says that God always gives:

> ". . . more to this soul; he shows it clearly his most sacred humanity in a way that he wills, either as he lived in the world or after being resurrected, and although so quickly that we might compare it to a lightning bolt, it remains so engraven in the imagination— this glorious image—that I think it impossible to dispel it until one sees it where he can enjoy it forever" (Mansions VI, 9, 3).

All this awaits those of us who will learn to "prize our souls as creatures made in the image of God deserve, thus we do not realize the great secrets that are in them" (Mansions VII, 1, 1).

St. Teresa reached an extraordinary knowledge of her own soul, and she can hardly be surpassed by the mystical life she led. But St. Teresa was preeminently a *practical* woman. And these intimate associations she had with God point not to any opposition between her practicality and her spiritual life. They rather show us the practicality and the realism of a life lived with God. It is we who live in a world of phantasy. Thus her great contribution to the consideration of the image of God in man lies not in the theoretical order, but rather in the field of experience. Her life is the greatest "proof" we have of the Thomistic exposition of the Blessed Trinity, and the doctrine of the image of God.

The Vision of the Blessed Trinity According to St. Teresa

Outline

I. THREE KINDS OF DIVINE GIFTS

    A. Perfect love
        1. Its necesssity
        2. In what it consists essentially
        3. How it can be attained
    B. Mystical contemplation
        1. In what it consists
            a. As distinguished from acquired contemplation
        2. Are there two ways?
        3. According to the "Mansions"
    C. Visions and revelations
        1. Their place in the spiritual life
        2. Types of visions
            a. Corporeal
            b. Imaginative
            c. Intellectual

II. THE VISION OF THE BLESSED TRINITY

    A. To whom it is given
    B. Doctrinal basis and significance
        1. The presence of God
        2. Grace
    C. The type of vision
    D. An examination of its constituent parts
        1. The Trinity as One
        2. The Relationship of the Three Persons
        3. The Humanity of the Word
    E. The communication of the Trinity
    F. Special favors bestowed on St. Teresa.
        1. Effects on her soul
    G. Purpose of the vision

Part I
Divine Gifts

"Without me, you are nothing," are the words Our Lord used to bring out our relationship and total dependence on God. We are debtors to God for everything that we possess. St. Thérèse brought this out very strikingly when she said, "everything is a grace." And, indeed, from the *"initium Fidei"* to the *"magnum donum Dei,"* which is the grace of final perseverance, we are dependent on the wholly gratuitous gift of grace with varying degrees of active and passive receptivity. If this is true of the Christian who strives to keep the commandments, then how much more true is it of those few who respond to the way of the counsels?

With this in view, St. Teresa, speaking of the spiritual or the "mystical" life, distinguishes three kinds of divine gifts: visions and revelations, mystical contemplation, and perfect love (Fr. Gabriel of St. Mary Magdalen, OCD,, *St. Teresa of Jesus*, Westminster, Maryland: The Newman Press, 1949, p. 96). Our book is directly concerned with the first of these gifts, but also indirectly with the other two. Christian perfection consists in the perfection of charity. And according to St. John of the Cross: "The soul is not united to God in this life through understanding, nor through enjoyment, nor through the imagination. nor through any sense whatsoever; but only through faith according to the understanding, and through hope according to the memory, and through love according to the will" (Ascent of the Mount, Bk. 2, ch. 6). The theological virtues are the immediate means to union with God; through them we are enabled to operate in a supernatural manner for they have as their object and end, God himself considered in his Deity. "But the greatest of these is Charity," for faith and hope will pass away in the next life, they will give way to vision, but love will remain. Union with God depends ultimately on the conformity of our will with his. "Theresa's moral ideal . . .; to give ourselves completely to God—to embrace suffering—to seek God's good pleasure at all costs—to set our happiness in the will of God, even

when this is repugnant to nature—is finally fully expanded in the
concept of 'perfect love' " (Fr. Gabriel, op. cit., p. 9). Perfect
love is absolutely necessary for the attainment of our spiritual
perfection, and in St. Teresa's teaching on the spiritual life, it "is
proposed to us without any reserve whatever, as the end to
which we must all tend, and which we are certain to attain if we
will it" (Gabriel, op. cit., p. 96).

But to attain this state of perfect love some contend there
are two ways—others insist there is but one way. This brings us
to a consideration of the second kind of divine gift given to the
soul in the mystical life according to St. Teresa—the gift of mystical contemplation. First of all, is contemplation necessary for
sanctity? St. Teresa emphatically says: "God does not lead us
all by the same road." And:

> "Thus it is because all in this house practice prayer,
> they all have to be contemplatives; it is impossible and
> it will be a great grief for her who is not; not to under-
> stand this truth, that this is a thing that God gives, and
> since it is not necessary for salvation, neither does he
> ask it of us under constraint nor think anyone will
> request it" (Way of Perfection, XVII, 2).

But the Thomist School insists on the unity of the spiritual
life, and every holy soul according to them is a mystic soul—
contemplation is the "normal" development of the spiritual life.
The main difference between the two views lies in the definition
of contemplation. To the Thomists, contemplation consists in
the actuation of the Gifts of the Holy Spirit, which are given to
every man in the state of grace, and they develop in us with
charity. But to St. Teresa "contemplation is a state of prayer
wherein the soul is experimentally aware of God's action within
it" (Gabriel, op. cit., p. 24). The Thomist consideration of contemplation is from the ontological point of view, and were we to
follow this view, it would seem that every soul who reaches
sanctity is necessarily contemplative. But at the same time this
school offers little explanation for the manifestly different
forms of contemplation. If this was all that contemplation
meant to St. Teresa, she would readily admit the truth of the

Thomist contention, for she repeatedly insists on the universal call to prayer and contemplation. But she also mentions a "short cut" which is not given to all souls. This "short cut" is to her the way of mystical union through gratuitous supernatural favors or mystical contemplation as distinguished from ordinary "contemplation" or the illumination of the spirit which is, nevertheless, given to generous souls and leads to union, but in this kind of union the suspension of the powers is not necessary. St. Teresa says, "powerful is the Lord in enriching souls in many ways and in bringing them to these mansions and not by the concept of contemplation is characterized by the experience of passivity; it is a psychological approach in contradistinction to the Thomistic ontological approach. St. Teresa then readily admits the truth of the Thomist stand, but she has something more to contribute. Father Gabriel says:

> ". . . the Teresian school has distinguished a two-fold way of perfection: the common way and the mystical way, that is the way of contemplation. The common way knows nothing of infused forms of prayer of the characteristic type described by St. Teresa, yet it is not wholly deprived of infused graces. The living water, to which God invites all souls, the enlightening of the Holy Spirit by means of the contemplative Gifts, is withheld entirely from the soul that generously prepares itself" (St. Teresa of Jesus, p. 43).

Father Gabriel concludes:

> "The distinction between the two ways, on the contrarary, by attributing to the mystical way the fullness of, and the common way of real participation in, both contemplative prayer and fruitive union, brings out more clearly how the very enlightening of the Holy Spirit may take on varying forms whilst yet remaining fundamentally one and the same. Hence we believe the Teresian doctrine may not only usefully complete but even shed light upon the modern Thomist synthesis of the spiritual life" (St. Teresa of Jesus, pp. 44-45).

Contemplation is not an end in itself, moreover, it is not

necessary, as we have seen, for the attainment of union or sanctity. However, it is a most desirable thing, for by this "short cut" we are enabled to reach sanctity much more quickly. And it is for this reason that St. Teresa calls it an "end," though not a final end, towards which we should strive with all our might.

Contemplation takes us out of the purgative way, through the illuminative way and into the unitive way of mystical prayer, which St. Teresa describes so aptly in the Interior Castle. In this work the first three mansions correspond to the purgative way. the fourth to the illuminative, and the fifth, sixth and seventh to the unitive way. In the Fourth Mansion we enter mystical contemplation, in the Fifth the soul experiences a transformation so that there is perfect conformity of the will with the divine will which constitutes moral perfection. The Sixth and Seventh Mansions show the development of this grace of union until it becomes an habitual state. The Sixth Mansion brings the soul to the Spiritual Betrothal, and oftentimes to extraordinary favors like visions and revelations. The Seventh Mansion is the peak of the mystical life where the soul reaches the union of the Spiritual Marriage; here "The Three Persons commune with it and speak to it and make it understand those words which the Gospel says that the Lord said he and the Father and the Holy Spirit would come to dwell with the soul who loves him and keeps his commandments" (Mansions VII, 1, 6).

St. Teresa speaks here of the mystical way which is characterized by the perception of divine favors. And this St. John of the Cross calls general and obscure infused contemplation or contemplation received in faith. Those in the ordinary way are never so aware of the graces that are given to them. And on the other hand, the mystical way does not mean the way of visions and reve900altions necessarily. These must fall under the extraordinary favors given by God to whom he wills, over and above infused contemplation. Therefore "visions are entirely accidental phenomena, without which it is possible to attain to the highest mystical contemplation" (Gabriel, *Visions and Revelations*, p. 62). Visions are but the outward manifestation of an interior grace bestowed on the soul of God. This interior grace is compared to the pulp of the fruit, whereas the vision is like the rind according to the terminology of St. John of the Cross. And they fall under the classification of "creatures" and consequently must go. Therefore, we must not desire nor ask for these extraordinary favors, and when they come, if they are from God, there will be little we can do about them. However, St. John of the Cross advises us not to analyze them, nor even to preoccupy ourselves with them, but on the contrary, to reject them. For we can never be sure they are from God—the devil too can simulate a vision—and then there is always the danger that we become preoccupied with delights experienced through them and become attached to non-essentials and lose the accompanying grace that comes with it.

"St. John of the Cross distinguishes three kinds of visions; visions properly so called, revelations, and any knowledge of them" according to Fr. Marie Eugene, OCD *(I Am a Daughter of the Church*, p. 265). These visions may have as their object either the Creator or creatures. That is, God, himself in the mystery of the Trinity or in one of his divine attributes or created realities either of a spiritual or of a corporeal nature. "Revelations consist of the disclosure of hidden secrets and mysteries" (M. Eugene, Ibid.). Knowledge of truths consists "in understanding and seeing truth and (with the intellect) of God or of things that are, were and will be" (Ascent, BK. II, 26, 2). This knowledge of truths may be divided into two: supernatural words and divine touches. Supernatural words are either auricular, that is, heard by the external senses or those heard by the internal senses which are either imaginary or intellectual. Finally, intellectual words may be either formal, where the soul is aware they are being produced by an external agent; or they may be formal substantial, which effect immediately what they announce" (Lagrange, *Three Ages*, p. 592). Divine touches which are attached to "particular and distinct contemplation"— (this is the terminology of St. John of the Cross which corresponds to infused or mystical contemplation) but which are distinct from infused contemplation, are directly ordained to the sanctification of the person who receives them. They are imprinted on the will and react on the intellect and consequently they give "a very elevated feeling of God and very delightful in the intellect" (Ascent Bk. II, 32, 3).

I have saved the division of visions properly so called until last, for this is what we are primarily concerned with. Visions may be either of three kinds; sensible or corporeal; imaginative; and intellectual. They are said to be sensible when they appear to the eye from an external representation (or when an exterior voice is heard). This type of vision may be either corporeal in form, or an arrangement of light particles. We will say no more of this type, for St. Teresa never experienced them. The second type is called imaginative "when God, in order to express his thought to us, coordinates certain images that pre-exist in our imagination, or imprints new ones on it" directly (Catholic Encyclopedia, Vol. XV, p. 477). This is the most common type of vision and may be granted to a person either asleep or awake, and when awake it is almost always accompanied by at least a partial ecstasy. It may be either representative or symbolic. "It is representative when it presents an image of the very object intended to be known . . , it is symbolic when it indicates the object by means of a sign" (Catholic Encyl., Vol. XV, p. 477). The clearness of the corporeal vision depends on our own will, whereas the clearness of the imaginative vision depends entirely on the will of God. St. Teresa once experienced an imaginative vision of Our Lord in which she tried to get a clearer perception. She said "desiring in the extreme to know the color of his eyes or what was his size, that I might describe it, I have never merited to see it, nor was it enough for me to attempt it, rather, I lost the vision altogether" (Life 29, 1).

"No perfect imaginary vision occurs without an intellectual vision which makes the soul see and penetrate its meaning" (St. Thomas, De Veritate, q.12, a.12). For example, the former may concern the sacred humanity of Christ; the second his sacred Divinity. The imaginary vision clothes the intellectual vision with living and resplendent forms, and they seem to St. Teresa, "in some way more profitable because they are more in conformity to our nature" (Mansions VI, 9, 1). St. Teresa's first vision was of the intellectual type which left her somewhat disconcerted until she was favored with an imaginary one. This is how she explained the reception of the imaginary vision:

> "When Our Lord is pleased to bestow more on this soul, he shows it clearly his most sacred humanity in a way that he wills, either as he lived in the world or after being resurrected, and although so quickly that we might compare it to a lightning bolt, it remains so engraven in the imagination—this glorious image—that I think it impossible to dispel it until one sees it where he can enjoy it forever" (Mansions VI, 9, 3).

The third classification; intellectual visions are manifestations of an object to the intellect without any dependence on a
sensible image. If the object perceived lies within the sphere of
reason, the intellectual vision takes place by means of species or
ideas acquired by the intellect which are supernaturally coordi-
nated or modified by God. But if the object lies outside the
sphere of reason, it takes place by the miraculous infusion into
the mind of new species. These intellectual visions may be
either indistinct and obscure where the presence of an object is
manifested without any detail as to its intimate nature. St.
Teresa says: "one sees nothing neither interior nor exteriorly,
because it is not imaginary; but without seeing anything the soul
realizes who it is and whence it is represented more clearly than
if it saw it, except that nothing particular is represented to it,
only like a person would feel that another is near her and because she would be in the dark, we do not see her. It knows
with certitude that she is there" (Relations 4, 20).

Oftentimes these visions are distinct and clear and here
there is a sort of intuition of divine truths. St. Teresa speaks of
a vision "where it is revealed how all things are seen in God, and
how he has them all in himself. And it is of great benefit because although it passes in a moment it remains very engraven
(on the soul)" (Mansions VI, 10, 2). Intellectual visions may be
of bodily substances—although St. Teresa could see no face or
form, but "here one sees clearly that Jesus Christ, the Son of the
Virgin, is here" (Life 27, 4). Or they may be of spiritual substances (this same distinction holds for imaginary visions too).
Under this distinction there are three categories: "visions of
hidden or future events, visions of the divine attributes and the
soul itself, and visions of the Holy Trinity" (M. Eugene, *I Am a
Daughter of the Church*, p. 256, taken from St. John's categories). Concerning the soul, Fr. Poulain says: "In the natural state
we are conscious only of our mental activities, and thence we
conclude the existence of our faculties. But God can raise us
supernaturally to a higher knowledge and show us our nature
such as it actually is, and can even cause us to see our state of
grace" *(The Graces of Interior Prayer*, Herder, 1910, p. 301).
We will say more about the others later on, but let us make it
clear—all visions, regardless of the type, are signal favors, but
they are only means and consequently may not be desired.

Can a parallel be established between the degree of spirituality of the vision and the degree of sanctity or mystic state attained by the subject? St. Teresa says in her life: "although the aforementioned vision (intellectual) that represents God without an image is higher, in order to last the memory conforms to our weakness by keeping our thoughts well occupied; it is a great thing such a divine presence be expressed and put in the imagination" (Life 28, 9). Nevertheless, Farges explains this by saying: ". . . intellectual visions are reputed to be the more perfect, because their object is usually more sublime . . ." (Farges, *Mystical Phenomena*, London: Burns and Oates and Washbourne 1926, p. 327). "This is why—especially when they are frequent or habitual—they are reserved for the most perfect, but never to the exclusion of either imatinative or exterior visions," as was the expreience of St. Teresa. The hierarchy of types of visions is indisputable, however, their correspondence to the perfection of life rests on mere fittingness. Nevertheless "intellectual visions of the mystery of the Trinity, point indisputably (from experience) to a very high degree of mystical union" (Lucian Roure, *Catholic Encyclopedia*, Vol. XV, p. 478).

The three divisions of visions according to St. John of the Cross, as is evident, are not mutually exclusive, but they actually overlap in many ways. For instance, revelations may come to us by means of visions or of words; visions may be either revelations or the greater understanding of divine revealed truths already revealed; knowledge of truths invariably accompany visions, and supernatural words may contain revelations; and finally, it is possible to receive them all together in one successive vision! But the division is still a good one, for in each there are distinct elements.

With this necessary introduction we will pass on to a consideration of our main topic: the vision of the Holy Trinity.

Part II

The Vision

St. Teresa in the Seventh and highest Mansion speaks of this vision of the Blessed Trinity. This is how she describes the soul who enters it:

"It is placed in that mansion by an intellectual vision; by a certain revelation of the truth, the Most Holy Trinity is revealed to it, all three Persons with an enkindling that just comes to its spirit like a cloud of the greatest splendor, and these distinct Persons by an admirable knowledge which is given it, the soul understands with the greatest truth to be all three Persons, one substance and one power and one knowledge and only one God; likewise, what we know through faith, there the soul understands, we may say, by sight, although it is not seen with the eyes of the body nor of of the soul because it is not an imaginary vision. Here all three Persons commune with it and speak to it and make it understand those words which the Gospel tells that the Lord said He and the Father and the Holy Spirit would come to dwell with the soul who loves him and keeps his commandments" (Mansions VII, 1, 6).

From this we must conclude that this vision is a grace of the highest order and bestowed only on those in a very high state of spirituality. Even in the Seventh Mansion St. Teresa does not forget the poor soul still in the state of sin. She exhorts her sisters to pray for these souls. However, she says explicitly, "We are not concerned with those here, but with those who have already, through the mercy of God, done penance for their sins and are in grace." But she adds: "we cannot think of something neglected and retarded but of our interior world where so many and such pretty mansions, as you have seen, have room enough, and it is reasonable that it be so, for within this soul there is a mansion for God" (Mansions VII, 1, 5). After St. Teresa had experienced this vision she marveled "to see such majesty in a thing so lowly as my soul." Then she heard these words: "It is not lowly, daughter, for it is made in my image" (Relations 54).

Having learned her lesson she then remarks in the Seventh Mansion "each of us has (one) but we do not prize our souls as creatures made in the image of God deserve, thus we do not realize the great secrets that are in them" (Mansions VII, 1, 1), which she has already said in the First Mansion—that "It is enough for his Majesty to say that it is made according to his image that we can hardly realize the great dignity and beauty of the soul" (Mansions I, 1, 1). The image of God in man is a basic truth of the Church and one on which St. Teresa builds her whole conception of the Mansions. To this doctrine are insepar- ably linked the two truths of Grace and the Divine Indwelling in the souls of the Just. God is so intimately united with the very nature of man that for St. Teresa it is totally inconceivable that man should ever expect to know himself much less God without knowing something of his own soul. Self knowledge grows in proportion to our knowledge of God and of the soul.

The person who has come to the state of this vision of the Blessed Trinity which is, as St. Teresa said, the entrance to the Seventh Mansion, then must in the words of St. John of the Cross, first of all have "exercised itself in the hardships and bit- terness of mortification and in meditation on spiritual things . . . afterward . . . it passes through the pains and straits of love . . .it tells of having received great communications and many visits from its Beloved in which it has gone on improving and acquaint- ing itself in the love of him so much that passing beyond all things and beyond itself, it abandons itself to him through a union of love in a spiritual espousal in which, as one already betrothed, it has received great gifts and jewels from the Spouse" (Spiritual Canticle 27, 2). From thence God brings the soul into the Spiritual Marriage between the soul and the Son of God, her Spouse which, in the words of St. John of the Cross, "is much more than the Betrothal because it is a total transformation in the Beloved . . . in which the soul is made Divine and God by participation insofar as it can in this life and thus I think this state is never without confirmation in grace . . ." (Spiritual Canticle 27, 2).

St. Teresa speaks of our souls being in the image of God regardless of the state—she mentions this both in the First Mansion and in the Seventh. Now it is important to consider just what this means. St. Teresa gives us the answer to this question when she says that "within the soul there is a mansion for God" (Mansions VII, 1, 5). Therefore, the image of God in the soul can be explained by the presence of God in that soul. Now God is present in all things in three ways. St. Teresa realized this through a certain vision, after which she said "that one cannot doubt that the Trinity is by presence and by power and essence in our souls" (Relations 54). God is present in everything as being its cause, so long as a thing has being, he is intrinsically present within it. According to his knowledge, God is present in all things, for whatever God knows, exists. This is called *per praesentiam* or *scientiam.* God is present in all things *per potentiam* insofar as he operates in all things. And, thirdly, God is present in all things *per essentiam*, because in him action and essence are identical. Through this essence he is present substantially in all things, as the immediate origin of their essence.

This threefold presence of God is considered by theologians as a subjective presence or, in other words, with God as agent. And since man is an incorporation of a Divine idea, as to his body, he is considered a *vestigium Dei*, and properly speaking, as to the spiritual part of man, he is called an *imago Dei*, because he is an image of the Divine spirit. This much, the soul in the First Mansion has in common with the soul in the Seventh. But St. Teresa said, as we quoted above, that she is now treating of those who "have done penance for their sins and are *in grace*" (Mansions VII, 1). The *imago Dei* now becomes a *similitudo Dei*, for the soul becomes elevated to a higher supernatural grade of assimilation to God. The soul is now able to perform supernatural acts, and a new presence of God is attained— called an objective presence of God or God known and loved supernaturally through the faculties of the intellect and will. So the key to the whole supernatural life is grace. St. John of the Cross reminds us that the Spiritual Marriage actually does not substantially differ from the union of God with the soul which takes place at baptism. The Spiritual Marriage is merely the perfection of the same kind of union, which perfection depends upon the correspondence of the soul with this and the succeeding graces received.

Grace is nothing less than a participation in the Divine Nature, and the justified soul already bears in himself eternal life, for glory is but the perfection of grace; there is a substantial identity between grace and glory, consequently grace is the basis for the vision of God in the next life, and also for the vision of the Blessed Trinity in this life.

For a better understanding of this, it is necessary to treat something of the nature of Grace and of its relation to the soul. First of all, no matter how like it makes the soul to God, it still remains a created gift; it is not the Holy Spirit as Peter Lombard thought, nor is it the same as the Supernatural gift of Charity. Grace is (we are speaking here of Sanctifying grace) a real accident which inheres in the substance of the soul. It is an accident for it is added or (more properly) educed from the obediential potency of the soul. The soul is a complete substance and anything added to a substance is an accident. But this accident inheres to the substance of the soul and not to any of the soul's faculties; i.e., the intellect and the will.

Therefore, the Holy Spirit differs from Grace and is related to it as effect to cause, or giver to the gift. And since charity perfects the faculty of the will whereas grace affects the soul-substance itself, they also are distinct. Grace touches the very internal substance of the soul. But Grace as an accident that inheres in the substance of the soul permanently is a quality. Under the genus of quality grace corresponds to the species of habit. Now there are two kinds of habit—operative and entitative. Grace belongs to the first species of quality, though it it cannot properly be called a habit, because it is not immediately ordained to action, but to a kind of spiritual being which it produces in the soul" (St. Thomas, De Veritate, q.17, a.2, ad 7).

Therefore, since grace is supernatural it follows that it must be infused from above into a soul which has an obediential capacity for receiving it. Therefore, it is called an infused habit. "When the Holy Spirit infuses sanctifying grace, the *habitus entitativus* imparts to the soul a supernatural principle of being, while the *habitus operativus* confers upon it a supernatural power . . . which may be developed into a facility to perform salutary acts" *(De Veritate q.27, a.2)*.

Now let us apply this doctrine to the explanation of the Vision of the Most Holy Trinity given by St. Teresa. St. Teresa says: "It comes to its spirit like a cloud of the greatest splendor" (Mansions VII, 1, 6). Concerning words coming from the Holy Trinity, she said that "they are in the interior of her soul, in the very, very interior, in a very deep thing" (Mansions VII, 1, 7);

"the essential part of her soul was never moved from that room" (Mansions VII, 1, 10); "the Lord, himself appears in this center of the soul" (Mansions VII, 2, 3); "the soul remains always with its God in that center" (Mansions VII, 2, 4); "It understands clearly through certain secret aspirations it is God who gives life to our soul" (Mansions VII, 2, 6); the soul utters, "Oh life of my life" (Mansions VII, 2, 6); "it understands clearly that there is in the interior someone who hurls these arrows and gives life to this life" (Mansions VII, 2, 6); "the soul is left in pure spirit, in order that it might join in this celestial union with the uncreated spirit" (Mansions VII, 2, 7); "the Lord puts the soul in this mansion of his, which is the center of the soul itself . . . it seems there are no movements in this soul on entering here, which it usually has in the potencies and imagination" (Mansions VII, 2, 9); "This center of our soul or this spirit, is a thing so difficult to describe" (Mansions VII, 2, 10).

It is very difficult, indeed, to understand, and even more difficult to understand what St. Teresa means by her use of terms. But it would seem when she speaks here of the center of her soul or Spirit she means this actual *soul-substance* where grace is infused—life from God—by the Holy Spirit, and where grace inheres. She distinguishes this soul-substance from the faculties—and she felt this to be true, for while she went undisturbed in this substance of the soul, "she seemed to have a division in her soul (Mansions VII, 1, 10). But in another place she seems to distinguish between faculties and soul, even within the interior part: "there is in the interior someone who hurls these arrows and gives life to this life and there is a sun from whence proceeds a great light which is sent to the faculties from the interior of the soul" (Mansions VII, 2, 6). Perhaps we can explain this through the objective presence of God in the soul, or the presence of God in the soul as known and loved. This can be either on a natural plane or a supernatural one, so that the soul and its faculties can be considered, either as natural or supernatural. Moreover, St. Teresa distinguishes between the Spiritual union and the Spiritual Marriage in this passage where she says the soul while in the prayer of union "enters its superior part . . . but making it dumb and blind as St. Paul remained at his conversion." "But when he unites it with himself, it understands nothing so that all the faculties are lost" (Mansions VII, 1, 5). But on the other hand, St. Teresa when speaking of the

Spiritual Marriage says that "Here it is of another order; now our good God wants to get rid of the scales from our eyes that it may see and realize something of the mercy that he does it, although it is through a strange way" (Mansions VII, 1, 6). So even though God affects by grace the very substance of the soul, he nevertheless allows it in the Spiritual Marriage to understand *somewhat*, through the use of the supernaturalized faculties of the intellect and the will. Compare the effects of grace, for instance, according to the *Roman Catechism* with that which St. Teresa reports of the vision of the Trinity. The catechism says: "It (grace) enlightens the mind, strengthens the will, and sets aglow the fire of divine love in our soul." St. Teresa describes it: "with an enkindling which just comes to its spirit like a cloud of the greatest splendor" (Mansions VII, 1, 6).

Now after discussing *where* this vision is received, our next question is *how?* St. Teresa says that the soul is "put into that mansion through an intellectual vision" (Mansion VII, 1, 6). Moreover, "All three Persons commune with it and speak to it" (Mansions VII, 1, 6). In another place she says: "the Lord appears in this center of the soul without an imaginary vision but an intellectual one, although more delicate than the aforesaid" (Mansions VII, 2, 3). St. Teresa affirms that this communication takes place, then, only through an intellectual vision, but sometimes she has doubts. She seems to be sure that it is *not* an imaginary one for she says: "I know very well it is not imagination because even after I try to restore the image I can not, although I have tried (Relations 5, 21). Again she says: "the matter of imaginary visions has ceased, but it seems that this intellectual vision of these three Persons and of the Humanity goes on, which is, I believe, a very much higher thing" (Relations 6, 3). On two other occasions St. Teresa seems to be in doubt how to classify the vision. She says: "Having just communicated on the feast of St. Augustine—I don't know how—I was given to understand and almost to see (but that was an intellectual thing and passed quickly)" (Relations 47). And again she relates: "Once being in prayer, the Lord showed me by a strange type of intellectual vision how the soul was, that is in grace in whose company I saw the Most Holy Trinity through an intellectual vision" (Relations 24). In this latter description she makes a distinction between the vision of the Trinity and that of the soul. It seems this latter vision causes her more difficulty when it comes to description.

How are we to interpret "a strange type of intellectual vision?" St. John of the Cross distinguishes between knowledge of naked truths (or visions) which come to the soul with respect to the Creator and those that come to the soul with respect to creatures. In this latter type St. John says the soul "is learning something else about a thing with the spirit it presently has about that thing" (Ascent II, 26, 11). Since the soul is a creature, no matter how divinized it becomes, it is therefore the direct object of human knowledge as Being. God is above the categories of Being, so he consequently is above human knowledge except through analogies and comparisons. Even when the faculties of the soul are supernaturalized and God is the object— they can never understand with any clarity, but only confusedly. St. Teresa says concerning the Trinity: "for though it seems they are not for our lowliness to understand something of them, there remains in the soul a benefit (momentarily) without comparison, greater than from many years of meditation and without understanding how" (Relations 47).

Finally, St. Teresa describes a vision in which God permits her to understand (insofar as human knowledge is concerned) in a greater degree than she had ever known. This comes about through an imaginary vision or one which is more in conformity with our lowly natures. She says: "one day after the feast of St. Matthew, remaining as usual after I saw the vision of the Most Blessed Trinity and how it is with the soul that is in grace, it was given to me to understand very clearly, in such a way that by certain ways and comparisons through an imaginary vision I saw it. And although other times it had been given me to understand by an intellectual vision the Most Holy Trinity, the truth has not remained with me after several days as it has now, I mean for thinking about it and consoling myself in this" (Relations 33).

This is only possible as she says, "by certain ways and comparisons," for the Most Holy Trinity can never be the object of the imagination, except through analogy.

In conclusion, we must maintain that this vision is knowledge, for only through knowledge do we enjoy fruition in the next life, but this knowledge is, nevertheless, an immediate contact with the Divine through an objective presence. Gracian explains it as a "vision of knowledge, born of Faith" (Peers, *Complete Works of St. Teresa*, vol. II, p. 331 footnote). Luis de

Leon comments on St. Teresa's vision which is described in the VII Mansion (Peers, vol. II, p. 331 footnote). He says: "though man in this life, if so raised by God, may lose use of his senses and have a fleeting glimpse of the Divine Essence, as was probably the case with St. Paul and Moses and certain others, the Mother is not speaking here of this kind of vision, which, though fleeting, is intuitive and clear, but of a knowledge of this mystery which God gives to certain souls, through a most powerful light which he infuses into them, not without created species. But, as this species is not corporeal, nor figured in the imagination, the Mother says that this vision is intellectual and not imaginary." St. John of the Cross uses a term called Divine Touches or Touches of Knowledge which seems to correspond to this type of knowledge, for he says: "this Touch of Knowledge and delight is nevertheless so sublime and profound that it penetrates the substance of the soul . . . that kind of knowledge savors of the Divine Essence and of eternal life" (Ascent, XXVI, 26, 5). St. Teresa and St. John quote in regard to this, the same passage from the Gospel of St. John—XIV, 21 aq.

Now we must consider the vision itself of the Blessed Trinity. There are several main points of doctrine which were impressed on the soul of St. Teresa. But before we say anything more, it is well to remember in the words of St. John of the Cross that "there are no more articles to be revealed concerning the substance of our faith than those which have already been revealed to the Church . . ." (Ascent, Bk. II, 27, 4). And even in these high degrees of knowledge, called revelations, Touches or supernatural words, St. John still cautions passivity for were we to actively work on them the devil could then intervene. St. Teresa is in full accordance with the Mystical Doctor when she says: "nor do I occupy myself more in asking for what God wills, for then it seems the devil might deceive me" (Relations 5, 21).

Through the vision she comes to realize as never before that the Trinity is Three distinct Persons and yet they are One God, One Essence, One Substance. This is the principle truth with which this vision is concerned. Let us hear St. Teresa: "the Most Holy Trinity is revealed to it, all three Persons . . . and these distinct Persons by an admirable knowledge which is given, the soul understands with the greatest truth to be all three Persons, one substance and one power and one knowledge and only one God" (Mansions VII, 1, 6). In the *Spiritual Relations* she relates: "The Persons I see clearly to be distinct, as I saw it yesterday . . . although these Persons are understood as distinct, in a strange manner, the soul understands it to be only one God (Relations 5, 22-23). After another vision she says: "I have remained from here on unable to think of anyone of the three Divine Persons without understanding that all are three" (Relations 47). In the most completely understood of the visions she says: "what was represented to me are three distinct Persons; each one can be gazed upon and talked to by Himself . . . In all three Persons there is no more than one will and one power and one Lordship in a way that one can do nothing without the other . . . for he is one essence and where one is, all three are; they cannot be divided" (Relations 33,3).

The next important point of doctrine is the relationship between the three Persons; this involves also the question of the Humanity of the Second Person. And it is in this mutual relation of the Persons to one another, and not in the Divine Essence, that the difference of the Divine Persons is founded, so theology tells us. The fundamental law of the Trinity is: "*In Deo omnia sunt unum, ubi non obviat relationis oppositio.*" In God all things are one except where there is opposition of relation. Now in the Trinity there are four real relations: The origin of the Divine Persons from one another or sometimes called the Divine processions which establish in God two pairs of mutual relationships. These are: 1) the relationship of the Father to the Son; the active generation or paternity *(generare);* 2) the relationship of the Son to the Father; the passive generation or filiation *(generari);* 3) the relationship of the Father and of the Son to the Holy Spirit; the active spiration *(spirare);* 4) the relation of the Holy Spirit to the Father and to the Son; the passive spiration *(spirari).* The active spiration does not form a distinct person because it is common to both the Father and the Son. Therefore there are three Divine Persons. But it is through the Divine Missions that we can better understand something of the Trinity. Mission has to do with origin and object, or the relationship between the *"sender"* and the *"one sent."* The temporal missions of the three Divine Persons are a reflection of the Eternal Processions: so that the Father *sends* but is *not sent;* the Son *sends* and *is sent;* the Holy Spirit *is sent,* but does *not send.* The Missions are divided into invisible and visible. The invisible follows the bestowal of sanctifying grace and is directed at sanctification. And it is common to all three Persons. The visible Missions are of two classes, "according as the Divine Persons who is sent becomes visible to men by entering into the Hypostatic Union with a human nature (the word made flesh), or merely manifests himself to men by means of a visible symbol (as the Holy Spirit descending in the form of a dove)" (Pohle-Preuss, *The Divine Trinity*, St. Louis: Herder, 1943, p. 250). The Son proceeds from the intellect of the Father and the Holy Spirit proceeds from the will or the mutual love of the Father and of the Son.

St. Teresa says of these relations: "It seemed to me that the Person of the Father brought me close to himself and spoke very pleasing words. Among them, expressing what he wanted, he said to me: 'I gave you my Son and the Holy Spirit and this Virgin" (Relations 25, 1). Thus she testifies to the One Divine origin, and the double Mission where both the Son and the Holy Spirit were sent. St. Teresa affirms that "These Persons love and communicate and know each other . . . In all three Persons there is no more than one will and one power and one Lordship in a way that one can do nothing without the other: however many creatures there are, it is only one Creator . . . whoever pleases one of these three Divine Persons pleases all three" (Relations 33, 3). In other words, works *ad extra* are proper to the whole Trinity, and within the Triune life there is distinction only of relationship. But if they are all indivisible she wonders "how we see that the three Persons are divided and how did the Son take human flesh and not the Father or the Holy Spirit?" (Relations 33,3). She admits that she has been unable to grasp this but at the same time she trusts in the knowledge of theology. We see the Persons divided perhaps in respect to their Missions, which is based on the Divine Processions. And the fact that the Son took human flesh must stem from the relationship he has to the Trinity—his filiation, and his visible Mission as the Perfect Image of the Father. Later on, she came to understand this mystery of the Incarnation but she still is unable to explain it: "Among them was how the Person of the Son had taken human flesh and not the rest" (Relations 56). This Humanity of Christ remained a problem to St. Teresa until the Lord cleared up her doubts. She says in Relation 18: "as I was accustomed to draw towards myself only Jesus Christ, it always seems it brought about a certain impediment to see three

Persons even though I know he is only one God. While I was thinking about this, today the Lord told me that I erred in imagining things of the soul with the image of those of the body; that I should realize that they are very different, and that the soul was capable of much rejoicing" (Relations 18).

So important is this doctrine of the Humanity of the Word that it is through an imaginary vision of the Most Sacred Humanity that the soul is brought into the Spiritual Marriage. We note that the Lord in the words of St. Teresa, brings the soul into this Mansion of his "which is this seventh before the spiritual matrimony is consummated" (Mansion VII, 1, 3). And though "to other persons it will be through another method" (Mansions VII, 2, 1), it happened to St. Teresa in this way: In mid-November 1571, St. John of the Cross broke the Host and gave her only half for Communion. Then Our Lord, St. Teresa says: "revealed himself to me through an imaginary vision, like other times, very interiorly and gave me his right hand and said to me; 'look at this nail which is a sign that you will be my bride from today onward. Until now you had not merited it; from here on not only as Creator and King and your God will you look to my honor, but as my true bride; my honor is now yours and yours is mine. " (Relations 35). And he added "Other words which are easier to perceive than to tell" (Mansions VII, 2, 1).

As we said in the Introduction, visions are oftentimes accompanied by locutions or intellectual communications. So it is with St. Teresa for she affirms that the Trinity spoke to her soul. In 1572 she says, "what was revealed to me are three distinct Persons, one can look at and speak to each one by himself" (Relations 33, 3). In 1571 she had said: "It seemed all three Persons were speaking to me and they were revealed distinctly within my soul" (Relations 16). But in the year 1576 (the year is important as we shall see) she affirms in Relations 5 that she knows "the Person who always speaks; the rest I cannot affirm. The one well do I know has never spoken. I have hardly understood the reason" (Relations 5, 22). How are we to resolve such a contradiction? Perhaps it was due to a lack of perception for she says in this last quoted relation: "as it has been so many years I have been able to observe (these things) I can tell it with this determination" (Relations 5, 21). Thus over the years she was able to better distinguish between the three Persons who are one God.

Moreover she says: "It seems to me the Principal one spoke sometimes, but as of now I don't recall very well, neither what it was, nor will I dare to affirm it." Further on she adds: "I do not recall having found that Our Lord was talking to me, except in his humanity and I say now, this, which is no whim, I can affirm" (Relations 5, 23). So we conclude that both the Father and the Son who SEND and whose relationship derives from intellectuality, are the only two Persons who speak, which is consonant with their Mission, whereas, the Holy Spirit whose Procession is from the Will of Both the Father and the Son and whose Mission is to be sent, is quiet to St. Teresa, but, nevertheless, participates in the Eternal Communication of the Trinity as a whole.

Finally, the three Persons bestowed special favors on St. Teresa. She says: "I should see improvement in myself in three things, that each one of these Persons has done me a favor: one in charity, one in suffering with joy and one in perceiving this charity with ardor in the soul" (Relations 16, 1). These favors would seem to be from the Father, the Son and the Holy Spirit respectively. "God is Love" says St. John, which corresponds to the very Essence of God, the Father. Joy in suffering finds an echo in St. John 16:20, "but your sorrow shall be turned into joy" . . . "Ask and you shall receive, that your joy may be full." This corresponds to the Son, And the last favor corresponds to the Mission of the Holy Spirit which is contained in the words of St. Paul (Rom. 5:5-6), "The charity of God is poured forth in our hearts by the Holy Spirit who has been given to us."

The soul once having reached this high estate, is favored with many graces which flow from the vision of the Holy Trinity. "My acts and desires do not seem to have the strength they used to, for great as they are, greater must I do the will of God and what may be more to his glory" (Relations 6, 5), says St. Teresa. "Attachment to no creature nor to all the glory of heaven" has she, "but only to the love of this God" (Relations 6, 5). But on occasion she speaks of desires which make "the soul want to leave this impediment of the body" (Relations 47). This vision is "not like other visions for it brings strength in the faith, in a way that it cannot be doubted that the Trinity is by presence and by power and essence in our souls" (Relations 54). "My mind ends with the consideration that God is almighty and as he wishes, he does, and thus he can do all that he wishes; meanwhile the less I understand, the more I believe and it gives me greater devotion" (Relations 33, 3). And since this is so it stands to reason that the soul should experience in this companionship with the Holy Trinity "a power which dominated all the earth" (Relations 24). And this is the reason also for the efficacy of such a soul, for Our Lord said to her one day that since she was his bride she "should ask of him, that he promised to grant everything to me, as much as I asked for" (Relations 38).

In conclusion, I will list the striking effects of St. Teresa's prayer after having had this vision and been brought into the Spiritual Marriage. And to the best of her belief these "effects and how it leaves the soul advanced one cannot fail to recognize" (Relations 5, 20). In other words, they belong to the order of substantial words—they effect what they say. "The first is a forgetfulness of self, which really seems it no longer exists . . . because she is totally employed in obtaining the honor of God that it appears that the words of his Majesty said to her produced an effect from the work which was that she should look after his things and that he would take care of hers" (Mansions VII, 3, 2). "The second is a desire to suffer greatly, but not in a way that disquiets her as it used to . . . These souls also have a great interior joy when they are persecuted, with much more peace," they bear "a memory and a tender love for Our Lord . . . which proceeds from the interior of the soul" (Mansions VII, 3, 4-8).

Now these effects correspond very well with the three favors bestowed on St. Teresa by the Most Holy Trinity mentioned above. Other benefits could be mentioned such as the lack of aridity or interior trials, lack of fear, and a great peace in spite of any cross they may have. This is the life of the blessed— a participation of the glory of heaven. But St. Teresa will not have us think that prayer and contemplation are sufficient without the practice of the virtues for arriving at this state, wherein the soul recovers what was lost by Adam. We must die working and loving. But why all these favors? St. Teresa says simply they are given us "to strengthen our weakness . . . so that we can imitate (Our Lord) in much suffering" (Mansions VII, 4, 4). "His Majesty can do nothing greater for us, that is, to give us a life imitating that which his so-beloved Son lived" (Mansions VII, 4, 4).

Jesus of Teresa

There is a mosaic above the altar of St. Teresa at the Shrine of Our Lady of Holy Hill, Wisconsin. It depicts an incident that supposedly happened in the life of St. Teresa. Teresa was walking in her cloister and encountered a boy. He asked her what her name was. She replied, "I am Teresa of Jesus." She in turn asked him what his name was. The boy answered, "I am Jesus of Teresa."

There are few saints who have so clearly outlined the importance of the humanity of Jesus in the prayer life of Christians. Today there seems to be a resurgence of appreciation for the human Christ. Our faulty catechisms do stress the person of Jesus as a prelude to learning about the truths of the Faith. This is good as long as the psychological and personal elements are kept in perspective. This is seldom the case.

With the ecumenical movement Catholics have become curious, and many theologians and exegetes have read and been influenced by last century's existential Protestant theologians, whose emphasis was more on "life as lived" than on life as it should be lived as Christians. Rudolph Bultmann was one of these Protestant exegetes who has made a great impact on "newly renewed" Catholics. To him, Jesus is merely the occasion to decide in favor of authentic existence, since he could not be known with certainty from the Gospels. Thus Bultmann talked not of Jesus, but of the Christ-event. This in turn required of us a commitment to the truth. From this has flowed an emphasis on commitment, responsibility, life, authenticity and personal values. This leaves the Jesus of History a mere occasion for something, and not a flesh and blood Person with whom we can have any relation. This would hardly fit St. Teresa's conception of Jesus as it is explained in her writings.

At the risk of repeating many of the things I have already said in these chapters about St. Teresa's devotion to the humanity of Christ, it might be beneficial to trace in a more orderly fashion St. Teresa's experience of Jesus, and show how important this aspect of her spiritual life is to persons dedicated to prayer.

There are many today who would write off such a devotion as belonging to the 16th century, and of little relevance to today's Vatican II Church. But can we limit the mystic's vision to any age if it deals with a truth of the Faith?

Within the already christological traditions of the Carmelite Order, it was St. Teresa who reenforced this emphasis on the person of Christ. Between St. Teresa and St. John of the Cross, there are differences in approach, but they are both basically oriented toward a spirituality of the human Christ. One theologian seems to think that St. Teresa's synthesis of Christ's humanity is much closer to that of the Synoptics, while that of St. John is closer to the Gospel of St. John and the Epistles of St. Paul. Perhaps this conclusion comes from St. Teresa's attention to the historical Jesus, whereas St. John is more apt to speculate about Christ's meaning and role in the spiritual life.

We have St. Teresa's own words about Christ's importance in her spiritual development. She says in her *Life* (XXII, 4), "I had been so devoted all my life to Christ." She was always fond of images which portrayed him; it was through such an image her conversion took place. She says, "It was of Christ very wounded and so devout that in looking at it, I was all disturbed to see him like this" (Life IX, 1). At the time she wrote her *Life* she also liked to combine her reception of Communion with looking at an image. "Especially when I was communicating, I would desire always to bring before my eyes his portrait and image since I could not seal him so engraven on my soul as I would like" (Life XXII, 4). As is often the case with St. Teresa, she either changed her mind, or was a little better enlightened when she wrote the *Way of Perfection*. Here she counsels against this: "Moreover, having just received the Lord, for you have this same Person before you, try to shut the eyes of the body and open those of the soul and look into your heart . . .If you have to pray looking at an image of Christ, what are we looking at? It seems foolish to me to leave the Person himself to look at his sketch" (Way of Perfection, chap. 34, 11-12).

From the very beginning of her prayer life, Teresa turned to the life of Christ. She says, "I had this method of prayer: as I could not reflect with my mind, I tried to picture Christ within myself and I found myself better off, I think, in the parts of his life where I saw him all alone. It seemed to me that being alone and afflicted, as a person in need, he had to receive me" (Life IX, 4).

It was not an abstract view of divinity she viewed, but a real person. She says: "I could only think of Christ *as man;* but as it is I could never picture him myself, however much I read of his beauty and saw his images" (Life IX, 6). Her concept of Christ comes from the Gospels themselves, and no other source. When speaking of seeing God in creatures she says, "It is an admirable way to proceed while not neglecting too often the passion and life of Christ, which is from where he has come to us and from where comes all good" (Life XIII, 13). It is evident that Teresa paid close attention to this, because her writings are filled with allusions to almost everyone mentioned in the Gospels. She talks of Peter, walking on the water, that woman who called in her neighbors, the Mother of Jesus, St. Paul, etc. She also consults the tradition of the Church, especially through the saints to assure herself that she is doing the right thing in relying on the human Christ. "Let us look at the glorious St. Paul whom it appears the name of Jesus always fell from his lips . . . I have looked carefully . . . at certain saints, great contemplatives, and they walked by no other road: St. Francis gives an indication of it by his wounds; St. Anthony of Padua and the Infant, St. Bernard delighted in the Humanity; St. Catherine of Siena and many others . . ." (Life XII, 7).

We must not overlook the influence of what she read from the many available spiritual books then in circulation in Spain. She mentions, among others, the *Life of Christ* by Ludolph the Carthusian (Life XXXVIII), the works on prayer by Luis de Granada and those Franciscans whose devotion to the humanity of Christ was well known. Among these were the popular works of Bernardino de Laredo, who wrote the *Ascent of Mount Sion* and the *Third Spiritual Alphabet* of Francisco de Osuna. (These have all been mentioned before.) Many of these works were put on the Index by the Inquisition, simply, as the Grand Inquisitor said, to ban "this unseemly vulgarization of the mysteries of contemplative love," because, "He did not want such mysticism for carpenter's wives" (letter from Luis de Granada to Archbishop Carranza quoted by R. Hoornaert, *St. Teresa in Her Writings*, p. 74). Such censorship would be scorned today, but it was precisely because of at least one of these books that Teresa spent a good twenty years of her life following the erroneous opinions of Osuna and others concerning her approach to prayer dealing with the humanity of Christ.

All Spain was alive with a new mysticism and there were as many false doctrines as well as true ones. She says, "As I had no Director, I used to read from these books, where little by little I thought I learned a little bit (afterward I learned that if the Lord would not show me, I could depend little on books)" (Life XXII, 3). As she relates, her difficulties began when she reached a higher degree of prayer. She says, "I tried to ward off all corporeal things . . . I seemed to feel the presence of God . . . and as one experiencing that profit and pleasure, now there was no one who could make me turn towards the Humanity, besides, in truth it seemed to me it was an impediment" (Life XXII, 3).

This is what Osuna wrote: "We find it written that it is fitting for those who want to reach pure contemplation, to leave behind creatures and the Sacred Humanity to ascend the heights and receive more fully a communication with purely spiritual things. Since it was an advantageous thing for the Apostles to leave behind for a time the contemplation of the humanity of the Lord to more freely occupy themselves entirely in the contemplation of the divinity; it appears fitting also that they who wish to ascend to a higher state do the same thing for a time" (Osuna, *The Third Spiritual Alphabet*, prologue).

St. Teresa was greatly troubled by this for she sought the advice of several confessors on the subject. We know she spoke to St. Francis Borgia and he suggested in her words: "I should always begin prayer with a passage from the Passion and if afterward the Lord should lift up my spirit, I should not resist him" (Life XXIV, 3). This paralleled the advice given her by Juan de Pradanos, a young Jesuit confessor. She says, "He told me I should make my prayer each day with a passage from the Passion and that I should avail myself all I could from it and I should think only of the Humanity and those recollections and pleasures I should resist as much as I could" (Life XXIII, 17). He also suggested a little penance. From this period on she began to improve both in prayer and in conduct.

She could not think of this period when she purposefully abandoned the Lord's humanity without regret. She said "I can't remember a time concerning this opinion I had, that it doesn't cause me pain" (Life XXII, 2). In chapter 22 (of the first paragraph) of her *Life* she discussed this whole problem concerning created things and the supernatural. She says these books, "advise us greatly to withdraw from ourselves all corporeal imagination that one may attain contemplation of the divinity; for they say that although it may be the Humanity of Christ, those who are already so advanced are hindered or it impedes the most perfect contemplation." She then quotes their arguments which Osuna uses and concedes. "this seems good to me sometimes" (Life XXII, 1), but not entirely. She is still a bit timid about her opinion for she says, "I do not contradict it, because they are learned and spiritual men and they know what they are saying" (Life XXII, 2). She admits others may be led by different roads, but for her she says, "in my opinion it is a mistake" (Life XXII, 2).

She discussed this same problem many years later (12 to be exact) in her work, the *Interior Castle*, and it is interesting to compare her more mature opinion and attitude with what she wrote in her *Life*. I will quote what she wrote at length, which is to the point. In the Sixth Mansions (7, 5) she says:

"It will also appear to you that whomever enjoys things so elevated will not make meditation on the mysteries of the most sacred Humanity of Our Lord Jesus Christ because he will already be wholly practiced in love. This is a thing that I wrote about at length in another place, and although they have contradicted me about it and said that I do not understand it because there are roads along which Our Lord leads and when they have already passed beyond the beginnings it is better to treat of things of the divinity and flee from the corporeal, but to me they will not make me admit that it is a good road." She then reconsiders; "It can be that I am mistaken and we are all saying one thing." Then she regains her assurance: "Take care that I venture to say that you not believe whomever tells you otherwise. And I will try to explain myself better."

Aside from her experiences she did have reasons for adhering to the humanity of Christ. But first let us quote her experience after two years of praying for deliverance: "Being at prayer one day on the feast of the glorious St. Peter, I saw next to me, or I felt (for lack of a better expression) that neither with the eyes of the body nor of the soul did I see anything, but it seemed Christ was alongside of me" (Life XXVII, 2). When asked how she knew it was Christ she had great difficulty explaining. She said, "There one sees clearly that Jesus Christ, the Son of the Virgin is here present. In this other prayer certain inspirations are manifested from the Godhead; here together with these, it is evident the Most Sacred Humanity accompanies us and wants also to give graces" (Life XXVII, 4).

Her reasons, too, are quite sound. The first of these is based on our very natures as creatures and human beings. She says, "We are not angels but we have bodies . . . meditation has a need to have support from what is familiar" (Life XXII, 10). Without this dependence, she describes her thoughts as wandering and her soul like a bird flying about and never finding a resting place. The soul is walking on air. The second reason she gives is that contemplation is, after all, a gift and cannot be attained by human means. To attempt to raise ourselves up by not using the intercession of Christ is not only presumptuous, but it is useless. To reach perfection it is not necessary for God to give us great consolations. St. Teresa indicates that he has done enough in sending us his Son to show us the way, through the practice of virtue.

This touches on the necessity of having humility. Teresa says, "to want to lift up the soul as far as the Lord raises it, and not to be content to meditate on a thing so precious (the Sacred Humanity) is to want to be Mary before having worked with Martha" (Life XXII, 9). Without humility we defeat our own purposes. When a soul makes any effort on its own to procure the prayer of union and "this little defect of a little humility, although it seems to be nothing, does much harm in desiring to advance in contemplation" (Life XXII, 9). We could add a further reason from her writings for adhering to this Sacred Humanity throughout one's prayer life, and this is based on the very nature of Christ, himself. Even when we are advised to withdraw from creatures, we must remember that Christ, although man, is not a creature. Teresa expresses this in this way: "What I would like to explain is that the Most Sacred Humanity of Christ must not be classed in this account" (Life XXII, 8). He is the Way and the Light, she points out in the *Interior Castle*.

There is one exception St. Teresa makes to this, and that is when it is the Lord's work itself. She says, "when God wishes to suspend all the faculties, as in these types of prayer . . . it is clear that, although we do not want it, this Presence is taken away. Then well and good it is . . . But that we, with skill and care, get used to not attempting with all our strength to bring before us always . . . this most Sacred Humanity, this I say does not seem right to me" (Life XXII, 9).

Invariably, St. Teresa's vision of Christ is that of the Son of Man, for she sees him both in his glory and in his role of Suffering Servant. She says, "Almost always the Lord revealed himself to me resurrected and in the Host the same way, if not, there were some times to strengthen me if I was troubled that he showed me his wounds. Sometimes on the cross and in the Garden and with the crown of thorns a few times. Also carrying the cross sometimes for, as I say, my necessities and those of others, but always in the glorified flesh" (Life XXIX, 4).

This last observation is of great interest, in view of today's theology with its emphasis on the Resurrection. It seems that St. Teresa experienced this humanity as no one else has since St. Paul or maybe St. Francis. She comments, "Being one day at prayer, the Lord willed to show me only his hands." Then she adds, "After a few days I also saw that divine countenance." She realized the Lord was leading her "in proportion to her natural weakness." She declares that "Glorified bodies have such beauty that the glory which they bear in them, and seeing such a supernatural thing confuses one" (Life XXVIII, 1-2). One day when she was at Mass, she saw a complete representation of the most Sacred Humanity in its glorified flesh. She has this comment to make about it: "I can only say that if there were no other thing to delight our vision in heaven except the great beauty of glorified bodies, it is especially the greatest glory to see the Humanity of Our Lord Jesus Christ; even there his Majesty reveals himself according to what our misery can abide. What will it be like where one enjoys such good from everything? (Life XXVIII, 3).

If we wish to reach the heights of prayer, the way of the Sacred Humanity is the road. St. Teresa says, "By this way he travels secure. This Lord of ours is by whom all good comes to us. He will teach the way. Look at his life, it is the better standard. What more do we want from such a good friend at our side, that he will leave us not in trials and tribulations, as those of the world do?" (Life XXII, 7).

Epilogue

This study of St. Teresa's writings, with special emphasis on her polished work, the *Interior Castle*, is not meant to break any new ground, or just to satisfy the curious. It is presented as an overview for the person who doesn't have the time or inclination to delve into St. Teresa's spirituality alone. Actually, the *Interior Castle* is not my favorite among her writings, because it lacks some of the spontaneity of her other works. But it does give us the essence of her spiritual doctrine. It is an orderly presentation of the normal stages a soul goes through as it grows in the love of God through prayer. And according to St. Teresa prayer is perhaps the only way to grow in love both for God and neighbor. Moreover, we are assured by her that our prayer is best made to a definite Person, and not to an abstract ideal.

Jesus came to give us a concrete object to love—one that our senses and minds can grasp, but one that certainly exceeds our human powers. Thus it is, that to ignore Jesus in a belief in God is rather self-defeating. To believe in Jesus is to believe in God. To communicate with Jesus is prayer at its best.

While relying on the Scriptures and the example of the saints, Teresa does not see Jesus from the historical past, but as a present reality, alive and communicating to each soul through the sacraments of the Church and through the people and events around her. Jesus is no abstract Christ-event, and it is not his message she listens to without total reference to his Person. Moreover, he is not a person somewhere outside, but one who dwells within the deepest recesses of the soul. We find him in our quest for holiness not in a castle in the heavens, but rather within the castle of our soul.

One may object to Teresa's lack of reference to the Christian Community, or the presence of Jesus within the People of God, as it is so often taught today. Her unified Catholic background and Spain's total adherence to the Church would make that superfluous. In her dealings with people, she was always aware of the Holy Spirit's work within them. Teresa's regard for the individual is but a reflection of the Lord's teaching. In the final hour the Lord is not going to reward or condemn a community or an organization. Each one will have his day in court. God will look at how well each has lived up to the image of himself found in each soul.

I trust you will excuse a certain repetition in these chapters and understand that we are coming at our subject from different angles. My bibliography is far from complete, but for the most part I have relied on what St. Teresa has written rather than on commentaries. Those who attempt to apply her words to today's psychological categories do not have my confidence.

Finally, it is my hope that you will not regard this work merely as a study, but rather take some inspiration from it, so that you may set out (or continue) on St. Teresa's tour of the rooms of her splendid Castle, and maybe even find the Master in the inmost quarters awaiting your arrival.

Selected Bibliography

Dicken, E. W. Trueman, *The Crucible of Love.* (New York: Sheed & Ward, 1963)

Farges, Albert, *Mystical Phenomena.* (London: Burns, Oates & Washbourne, 1926)

Gabriel of St. Mary Magdalen, OCD, *St. Teresa of Jesus.* (Westminister, Maryland: The Newman Press, 1949)

Gabriel of St. Mary Magdalen, OCD, *Visions and Revelations.* (Westminster, Maryland: The Newman Press, 1950)

Hoornaert, Abbe Rodolphe, *St. Teresa in Her Writings.* (New York: Benziger Brothers, 1931)

Kieran Kavanaugh, OCD and Otilio Rodriguez, OCD, *The Collected Works of St. Teresa of Avila.* (Washington, DC: ICS Publications, 1976-1985)

La Grange, Garrigou, OP, *Three Ages of the Spiritual Life.* (Chicago: Herder, 1950)

Marie Eugene, OCD, *I Am A Daughter of the Church.* (Chicago: Fides Publishers Assoc., 1955)

Peers, E. Allison, *Complete Works of St. Teresa of Jesus.* (London: Sheed and Ward, 1944-1946)

Peers, E. Allison, *Complete Works of St. John of the Cross.* (Westminster, Maryland: Newman Press, 1946)

Pohle-Preuss, *The Divine Trinity.* (St. Louis: Herder, 1943)

St. Thomas Aquinas, *Summa Theologica*, 5 vols. (Westminster, Maryland, Christian Classics, 1981)

Tomas de la Cruz, OCD, *Obras de Santa Teresa de Jesus.* (Burgos: El Monte Carmelo, 1971)

Author's Biography

Nov. 23, 1929 - born in Harrisburg, Pennsylvania, but grew up on a Maryland farm

1946	graduated from public high school
1947	studied Spanish at American School of Mexico
1948	studied engineering at University of Maryland
1949	studied humanities at Fairfield University, Conn.
1951	entered Trappists at Gethsemani, KY. Left.
1952-53	two years in U.S. Navy, studied aerography
1953	entered Discalced Carmelite Novitiate, Brookline, Mass. Simple Profession, August 15, 1954, under the name of Fray Teresius of Jesus
1954-57	studied philosophy and humanities at Holy Hill, Wisconsin. Bachelors degree thesis: *Philosophy of Poetry*. Solemn Profession on August 15, 1957
1957-61	studied theology at Our Lady of Mount Carmel College of Theology, Wash. D.C. Masters Degree thesis: *De Origine hominis.* Ordained a priest on June 3, 1961.
1961-64	studied at Boston College and taught at St. Joseph's Minor Seminary, Peterborough, N.H. Also associate editor and poetry editor of *Spiritual Life Magazine*
1964-65	attended graduate school at Universidad de las Americas, Mexico
1966-67	taught English at Seminario Menor, Medellín Colombia
1968	Masters Degree thesis: *La Esperanza y la Memoria en la doctrina de San Juan de la Cruz.*
1968-75	helped found The Common Retreat House at Peterborough, New Hampshire
1970	helped set up Carmelite Desert in Hinton, W.V.
1975-79	lived eremitical life at Sharon, N.H.
1979	started Carmelite hermitage under Bishop Treinen in Leadore, Idaho
1980-95	Administrator of St. Joseph Mission Church in Leadore, Idaho
1985-95	Left Discalced Carmelite Order to found Public Association of Hermits of Mount Carmel, eremitical institute under Bishop of Boise, Lemhi, Idaho. Constructing hermitage complex from historic log buildings.

144

Current Books from Wenzel Press

THE BIBLE MAY AGREE WITH EVOLUTION, AND SCIENCE MAY AGREE WITH THE FLOOD. 122 illustrations including 23 full-page B&W photos. Offers proof that the Bible never disagrees with evolution. Doesn't conflict with Pope Pius' encyclical on evolution. Offers 10 chapters of possible proof for the world-wide flood, and includes scientific proof that God exists.

RUNNING FREE. 237 poems by Sebastian Temple, world-famous composer of the *Prayer of St. Francis* and other Catholic songs. His first book of rhythmic, rhyming poems is powerful, thought-provoking and deeply prayerful. Many of his poems end with surprising insights.

ST. TERESA'S CASTLE OF THE SOUL: A STUDY OF THE INTERIOR CASTLE. Explains St. Teresa's teachings on prayer by taking a few chapters at a time of the *Interior Castle*, but also comparing it constantly with all her other writings. Includes analysis of her writing style, the times she lived in, and adds three doctrinal studies of her visions.

ST. JOHN OF THE CROSS AND THE DARK NIGHT: *Understanding His Ascent and Dark Night in Easy Stages.* Explains St. John's books on prayer, taking a few chapters at a time. Completes St. John's outlines when St. John doesn't complete them himself. Includes 11 full-page B&W photos of peaceful mountain scenes to add to the meditative mood.

ASCENT OF THE MOUNT: THE LIFE AND WORKS OF ST. JOHN OF THE CROSS, 90-minute color video. Describes St. John's dramatic 16th-century life with hundreds of scenes depicting his life. Quotes his beautiful poetry which uses nature scenes to describe prayer, with 40 strikingly beautiful nature scenes to illustrate them. Video praised world wide.

HOMILIES FOR LIVING THE FAITH. Challenging homilies by a Carmelite hermit priest, covering the three-year cycle of Sundays. Always discusses the appropriate Scripture passages and includes little-known facts and history, inspiring the reader/listener to consult the Scriptures. Never uses personal experiences or condemns the past to push something new.

FOLK DANCE PHOTOS OF THE WORLD (other than Europe), with National Costume Index. 50 full-page B&W photos of dance performances of the Americas, Africa, Asia and South Seas. Also describes an amazing similarity between many of the folk dances of the world, but includes the many special differences they have. Then the back of the book lists an extensive list of where published pictures of national costumes are found in hundreds of magazines and books for all countries except Europe. Included is whether the published pictures are in color of male, female, bridal or court costumes.

FOLK DANCE PHOTOS OF EUROPE, with National Costumes Index. 50 full-page B&W photos of dance performances of Europe. Also describes the remarkable similarities between all European folk dances, but points out the very interesting differences each country has. Then the back of the book lists an extensive list of where published pictures of national costumes can be found for every European country, dividing the countries by Provinces, and even lists bridal costumes.

CLASSICAL AND FERTILITY DANCE PHOTOS, with Dance Costume Index. 50 full-page B&W photos of dance performances of the many spectacular classical dances of Asia, the flamenco dances of Spain, and the competition dances of Ireland and Scotland. Photos of fertility dances include grass-skirted costumes, feathered headdresses and masked dances (all danced to make their crops fertile). Also includes important new discoveries about the origins of these dances, as well as lists where published pictures of these dances can be found. (All the above three books have photos of actual dance performances that were taken only around Los Angeles County.)

ROME'S RUIN BY LEAD POISON. 24 illustrations. Offers proof that the decline of genius in Rome was due to use of lead, especially in wine, and mostly used by the upper class who thus became sterile and were the only ones with opportunity for higher education and advancement of the arts. Impressively documented. A Foreword is included by one of the country's leading authorities on lead poisoning.

Write for a free catalog to:

WENZEL PRESS
P. O. Box 14789-B
Long Beach, CA 90803